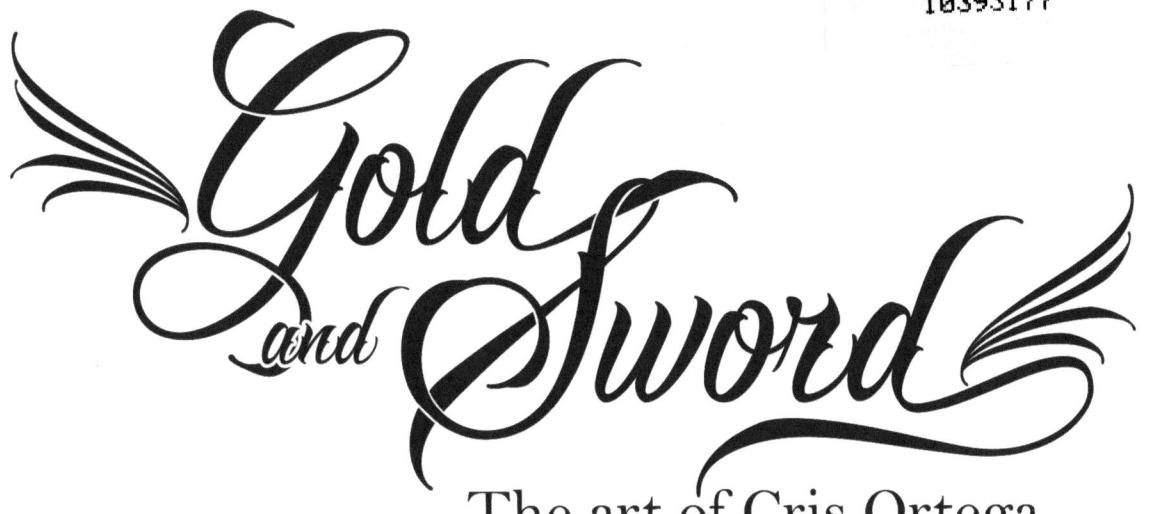

Gold and Sword

The art of Cris Ortega

Gold and Sword
© Cris Ortega, 2018

ISBN: 978-1545144923

Find more about the author at **www.crisortega.com**

Introduction

'Gold and Sword' is an art book whose pages contain a selection of old and recent works. Within this book you will find personal artworks mixed with commissions, some of them never published before, and the most prominent images that were included on the book 'Nocturna', only available in spanish until now. With genres that go from the most classic fantasy to science fiction, steampunk, gothic and romanticism, this book is filled with more than forty artworks for you to enjoy.

I invite you to turn the page and inmerse yourself in a fantasy world in which the beauty of the gold and the edge of the sword are woven together to form countless stories.

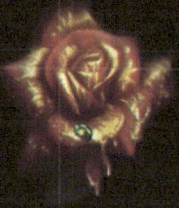

Introducción

'Gold and Sword' es un libro recopilatorio en el que se reune una selección de obras realizadas en los últimos años. En las siguientes páginas encontrarás ilustraciones cuya temática va desde la fantasía más clásica a la ciencia ficción, pasando por el steampunk, el gótico y el romanticismo. Obras personales se mezclan con imágenes de encargo, publicadas o inéditas, junto con las obras más destacadas que en su día formaron parte del libro 'Nocturna'.

Te invito a pasar la página y sumergirte en un mundo de fantasía en el que la belleza del oro y el filo de la espada se entrelazan para formar un sinfín de historias.

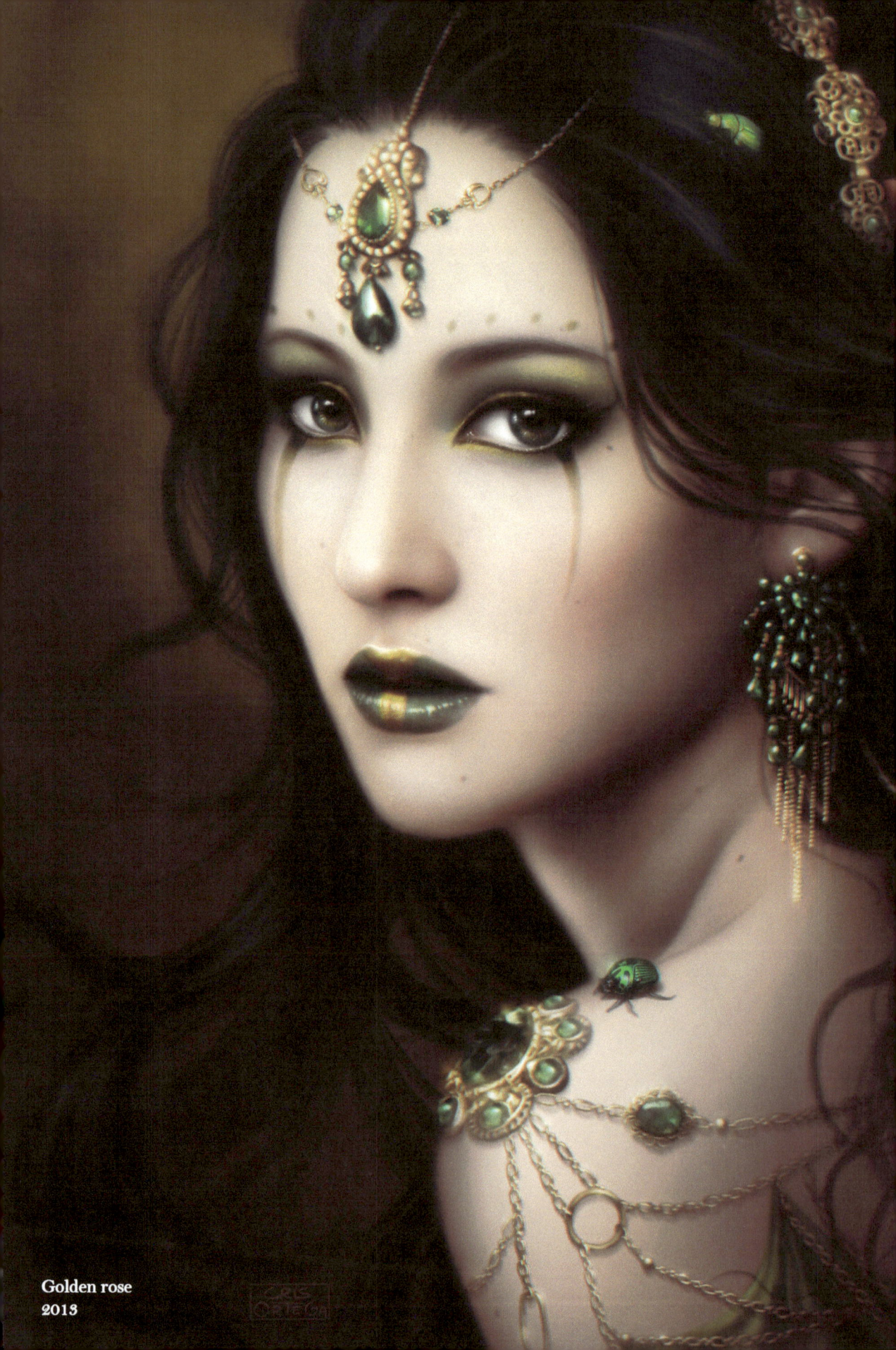

Golden rose
2013

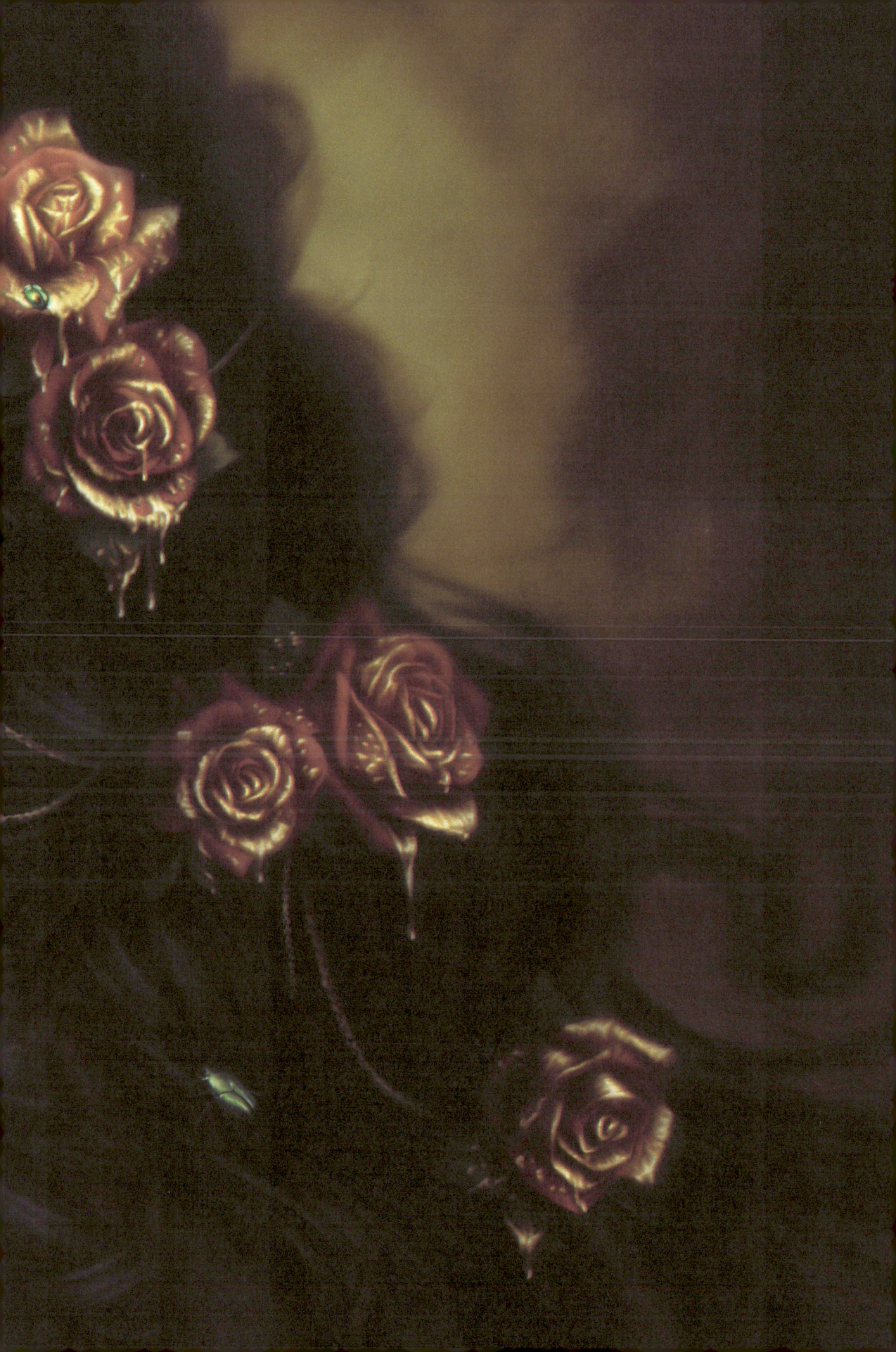

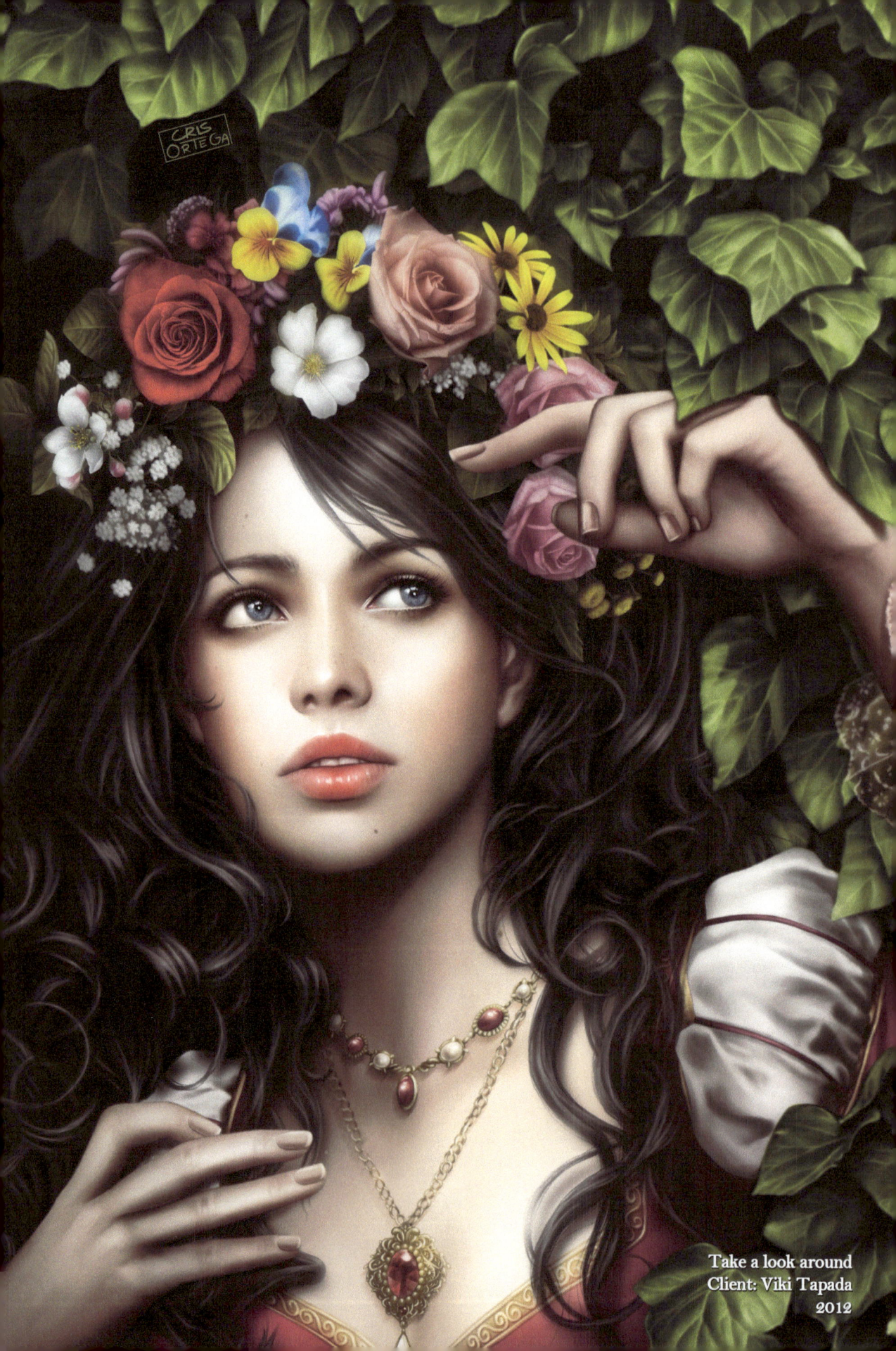

Take a look around
Client: Viki Tapada
2012

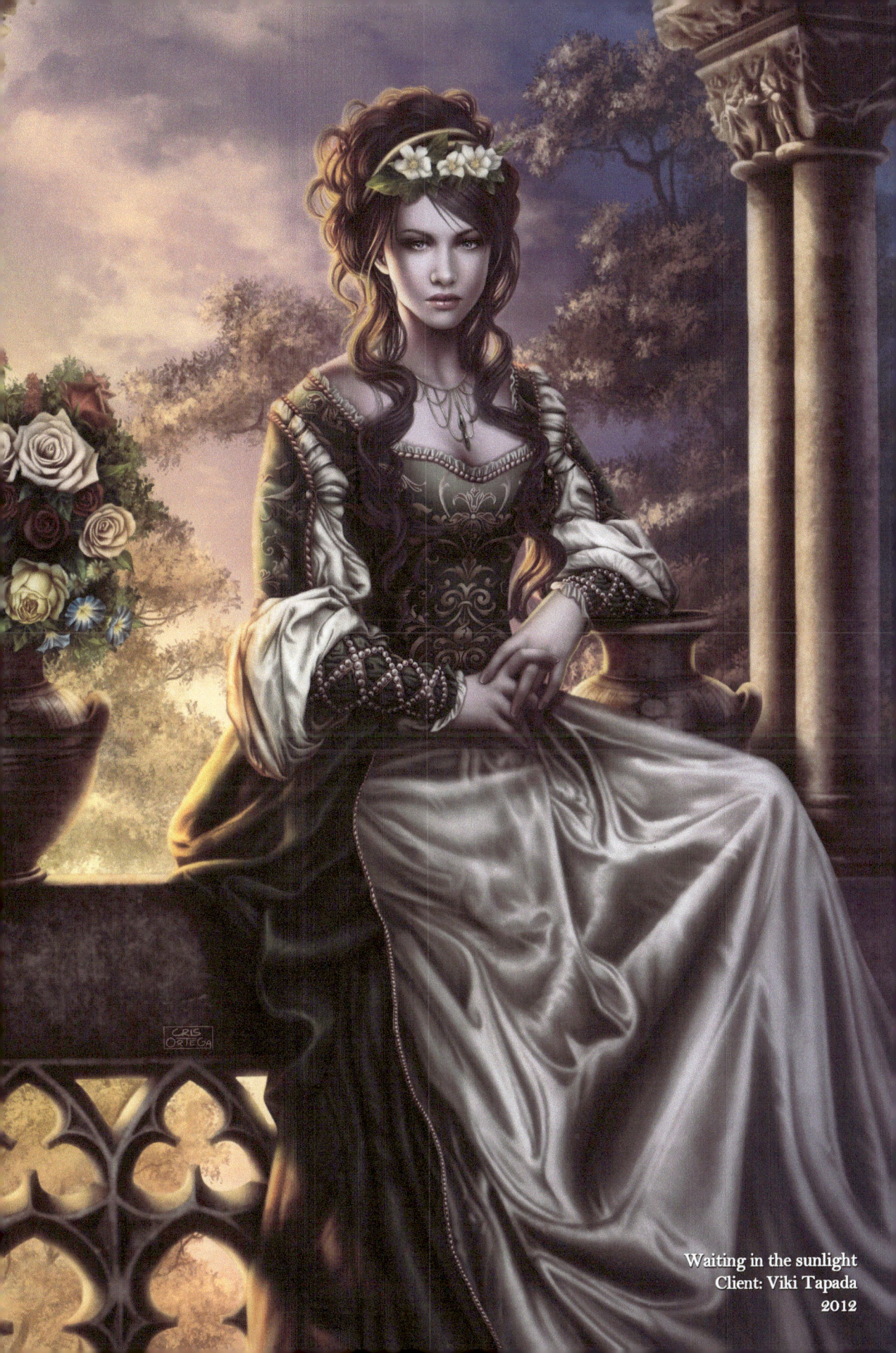

Waiting in the sunlight
Client: Viki Tapada
2012

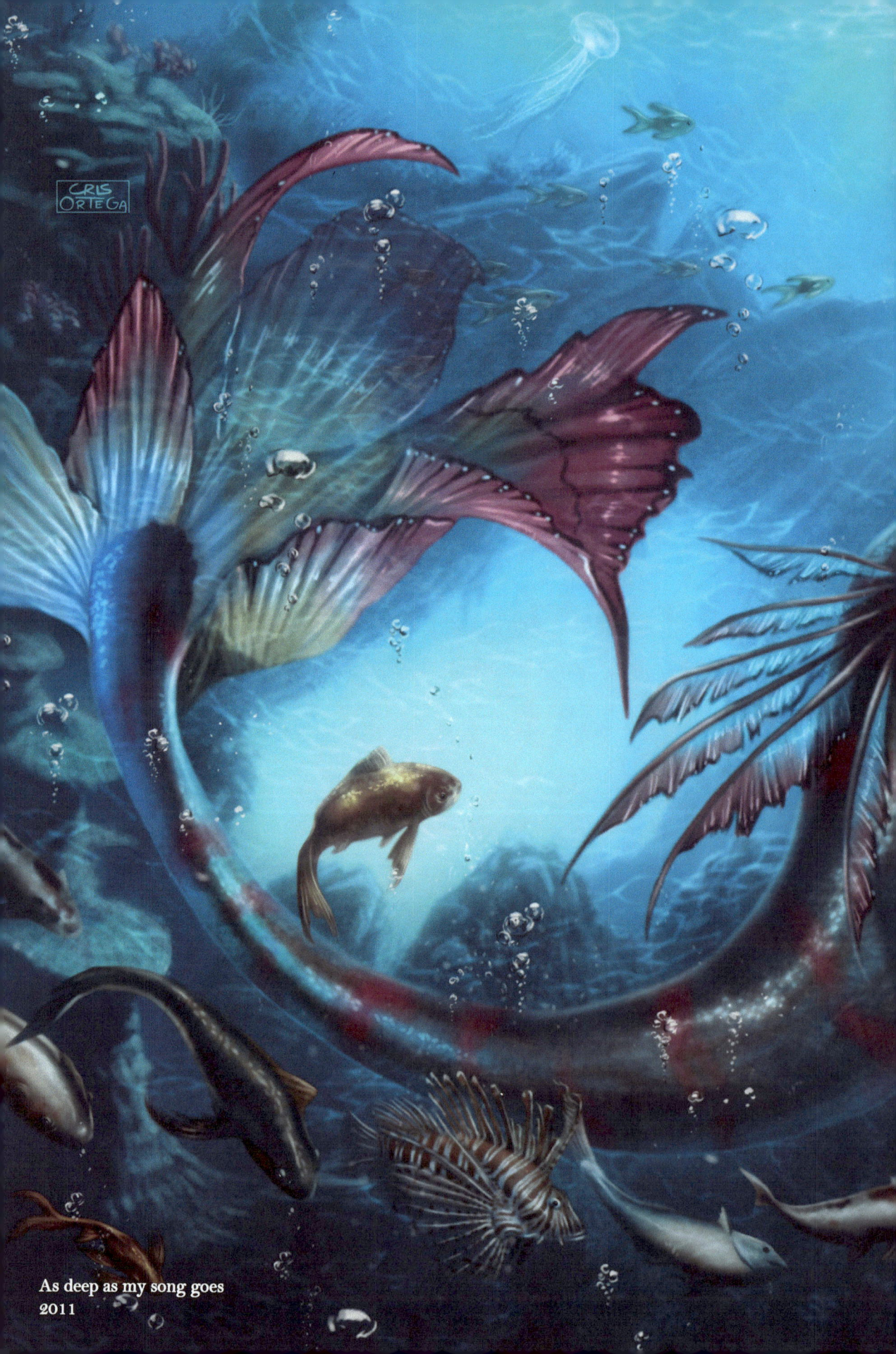

As deep as my song goes
2011

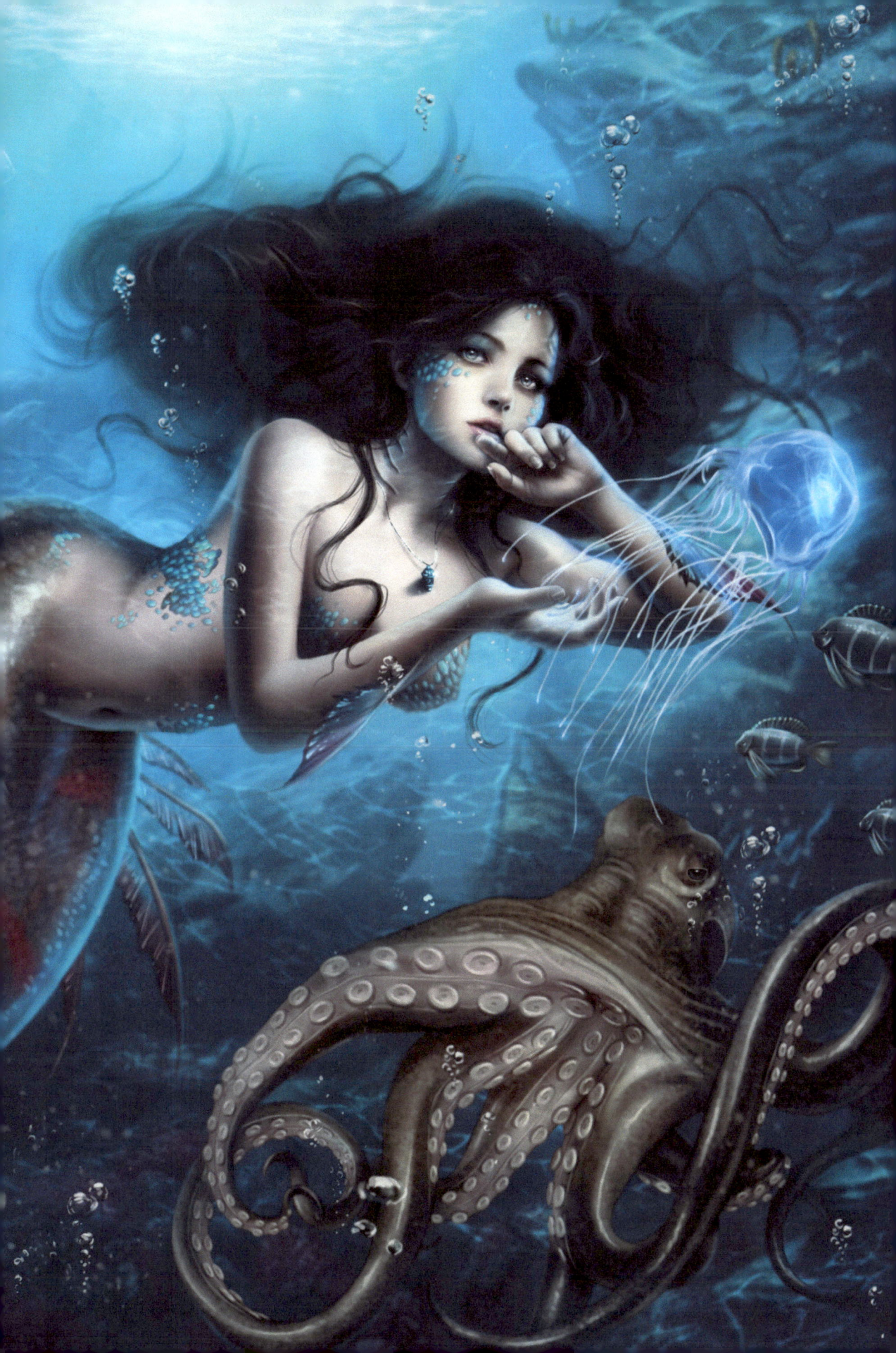

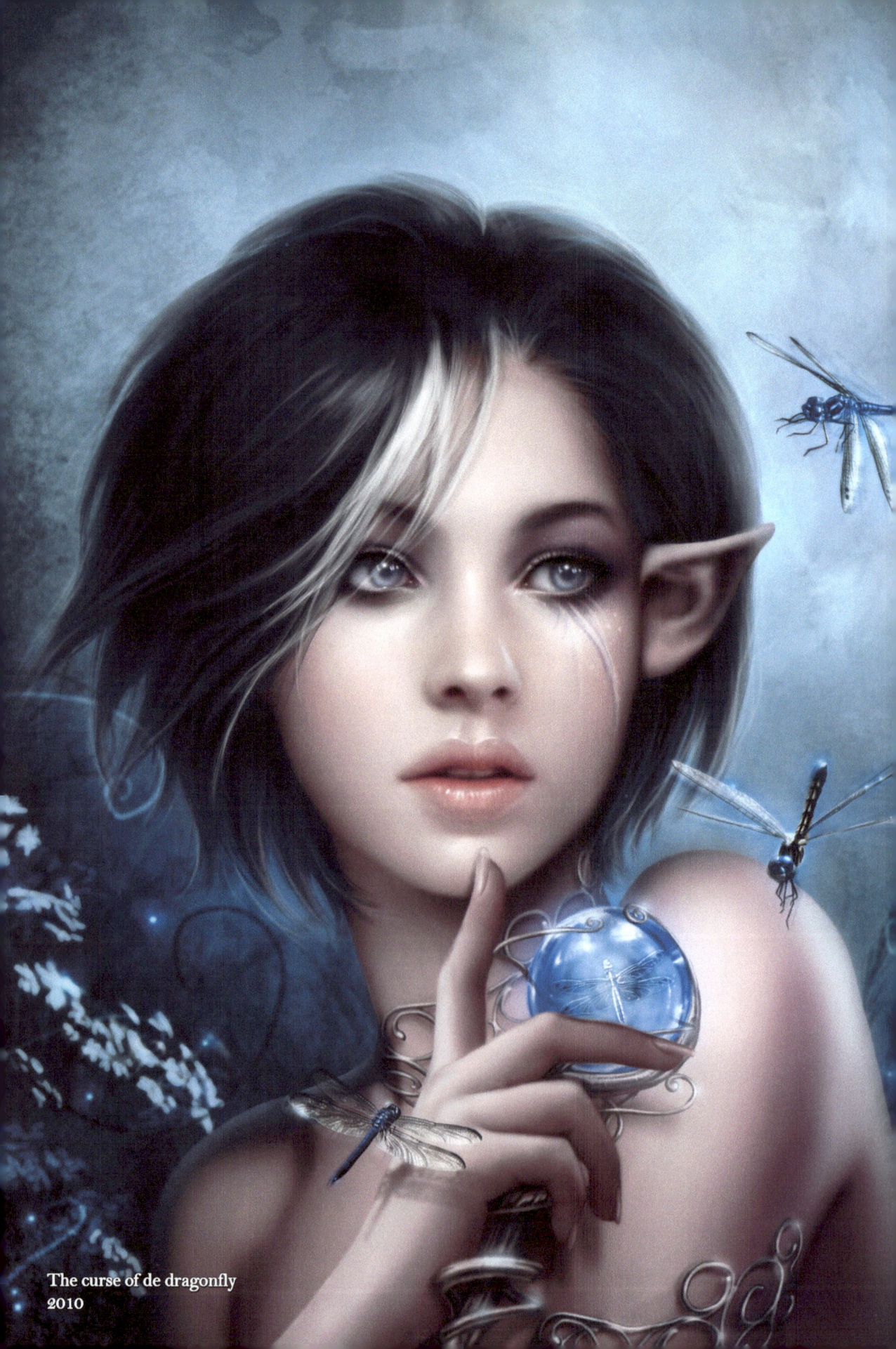

The curse of de dragonfly
2010

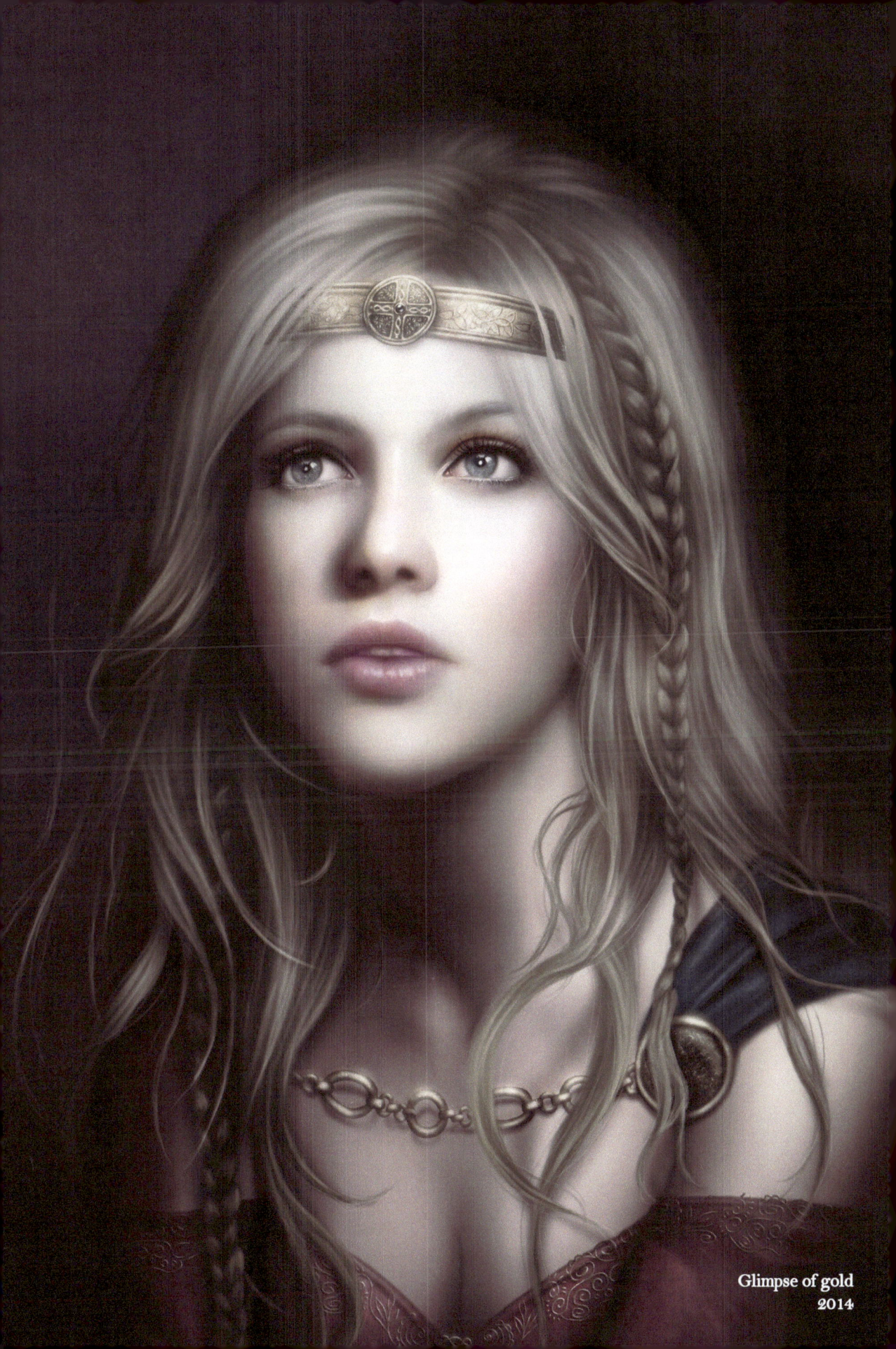

Glimpse of gold
2014

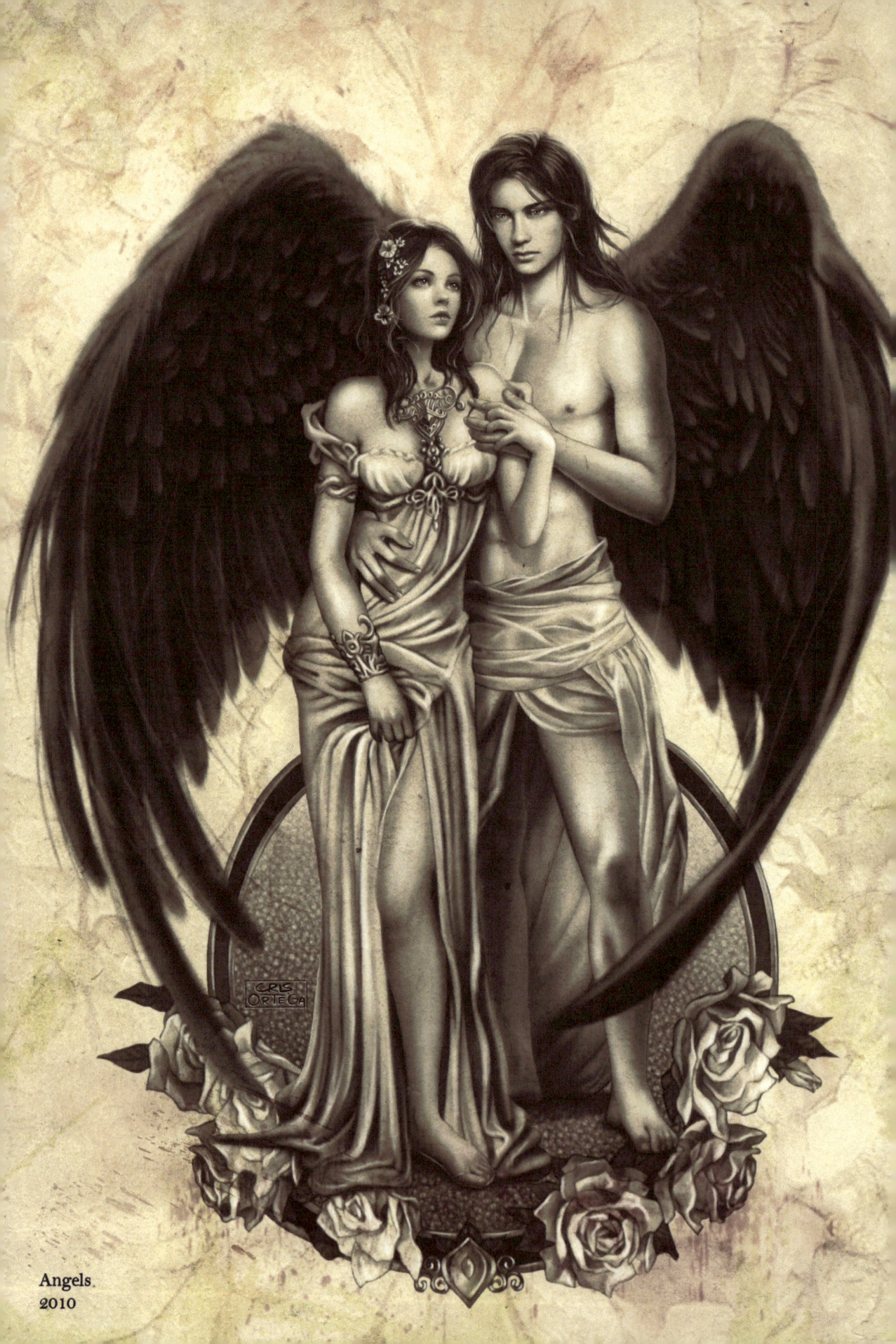

Angels.
2010

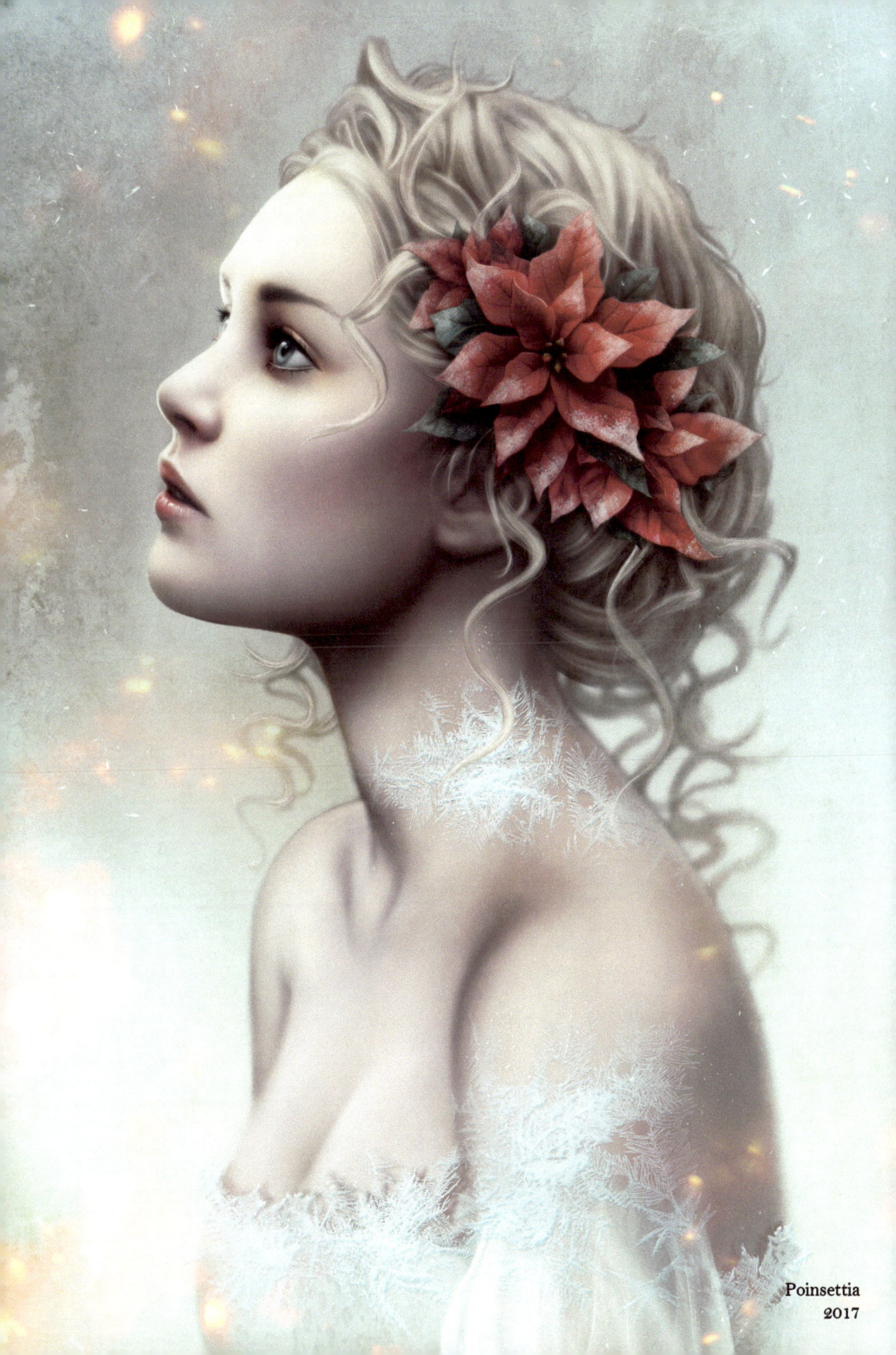

Poinsettia
2017

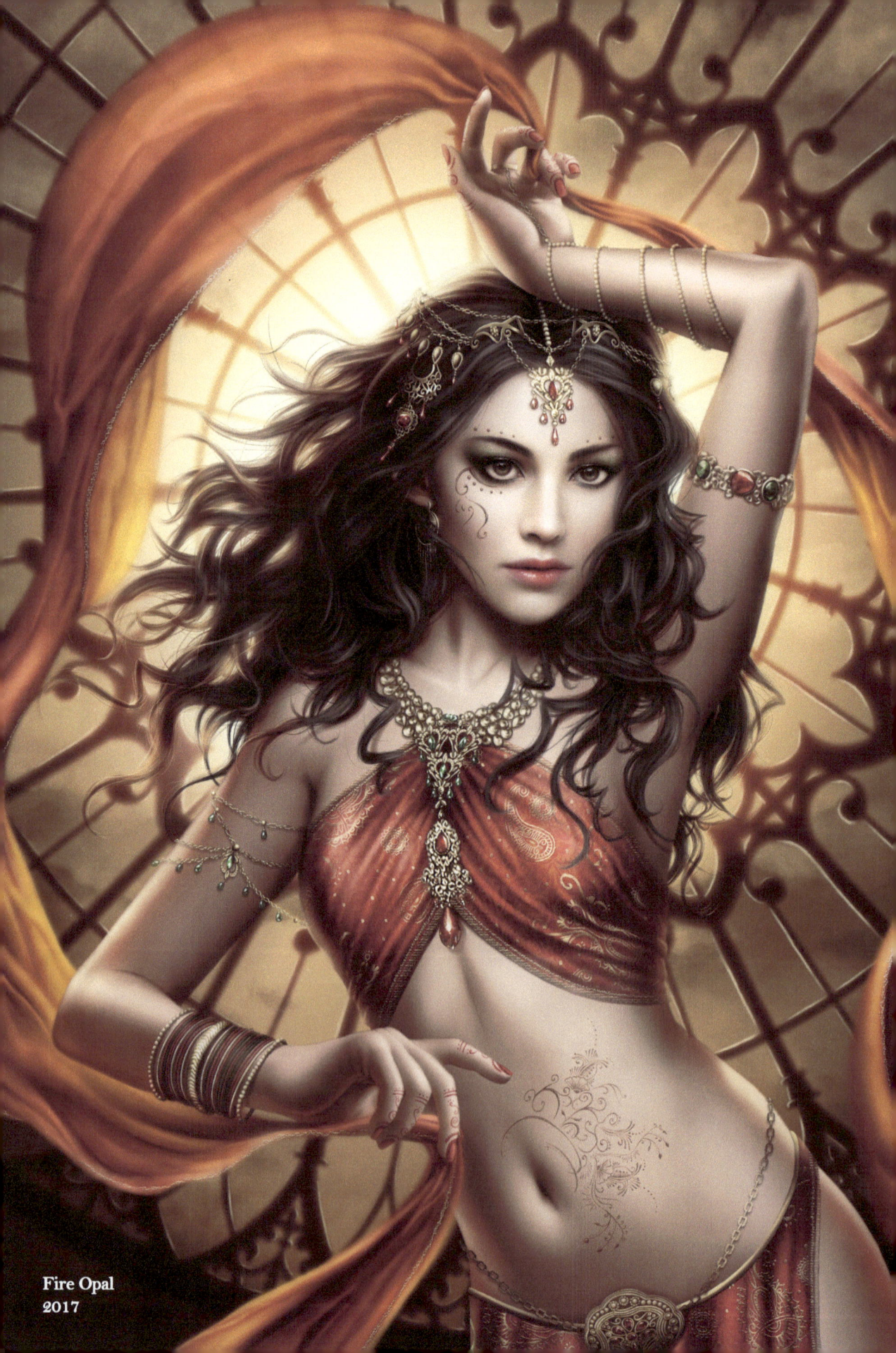

Fire Opal
2017

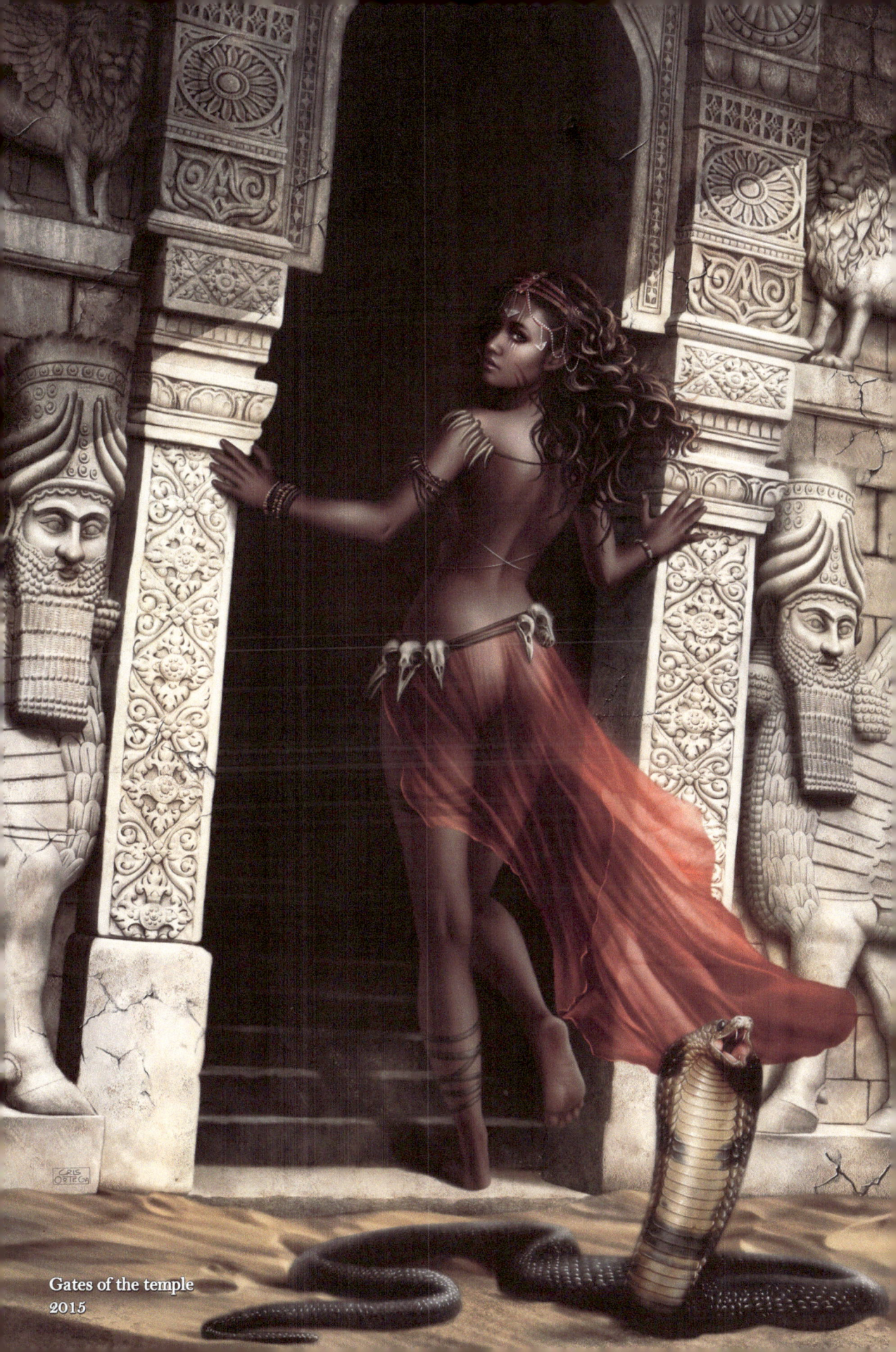

Gates of the temple
2015

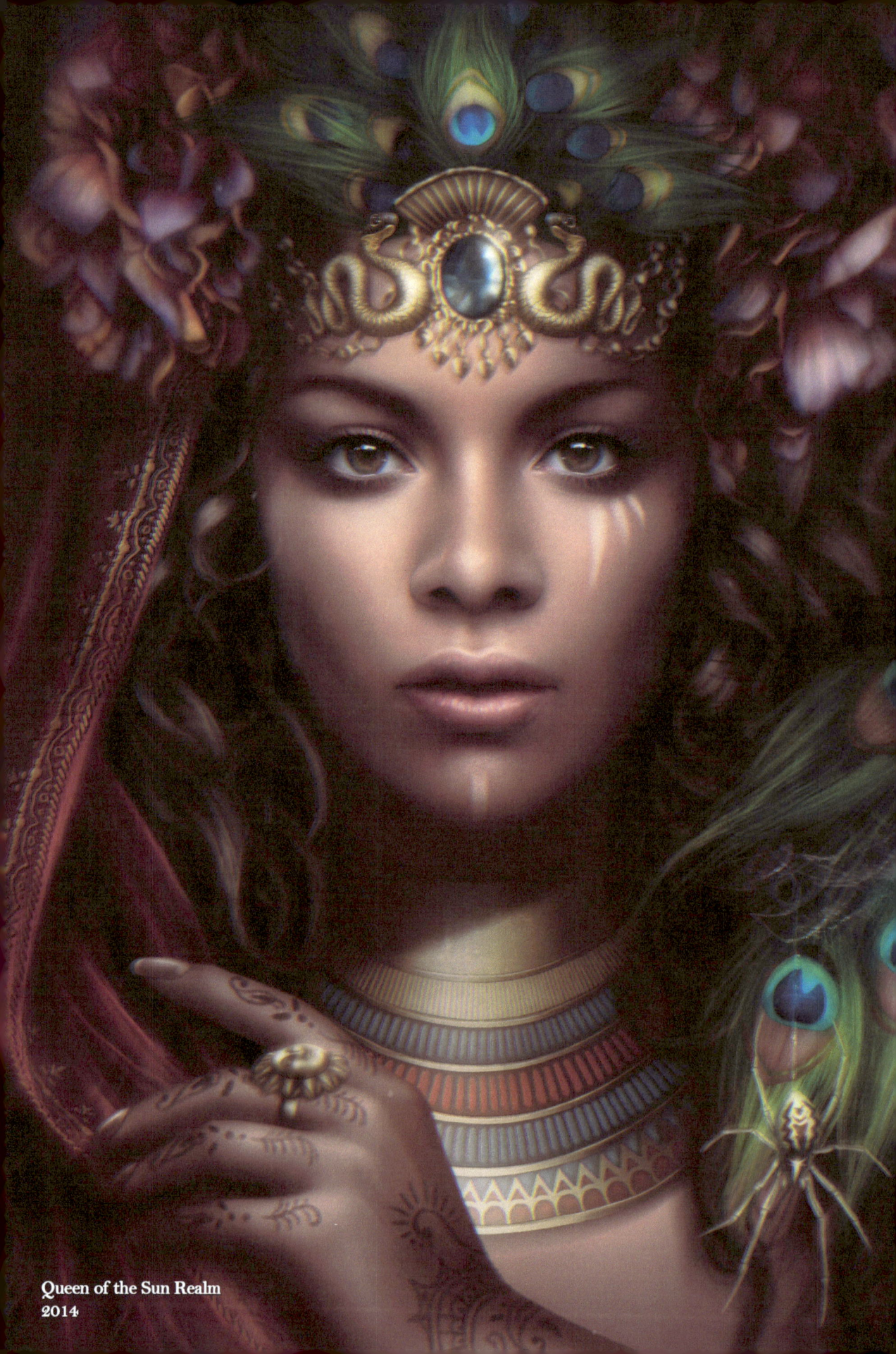

Queen of the Sun Realm
2014

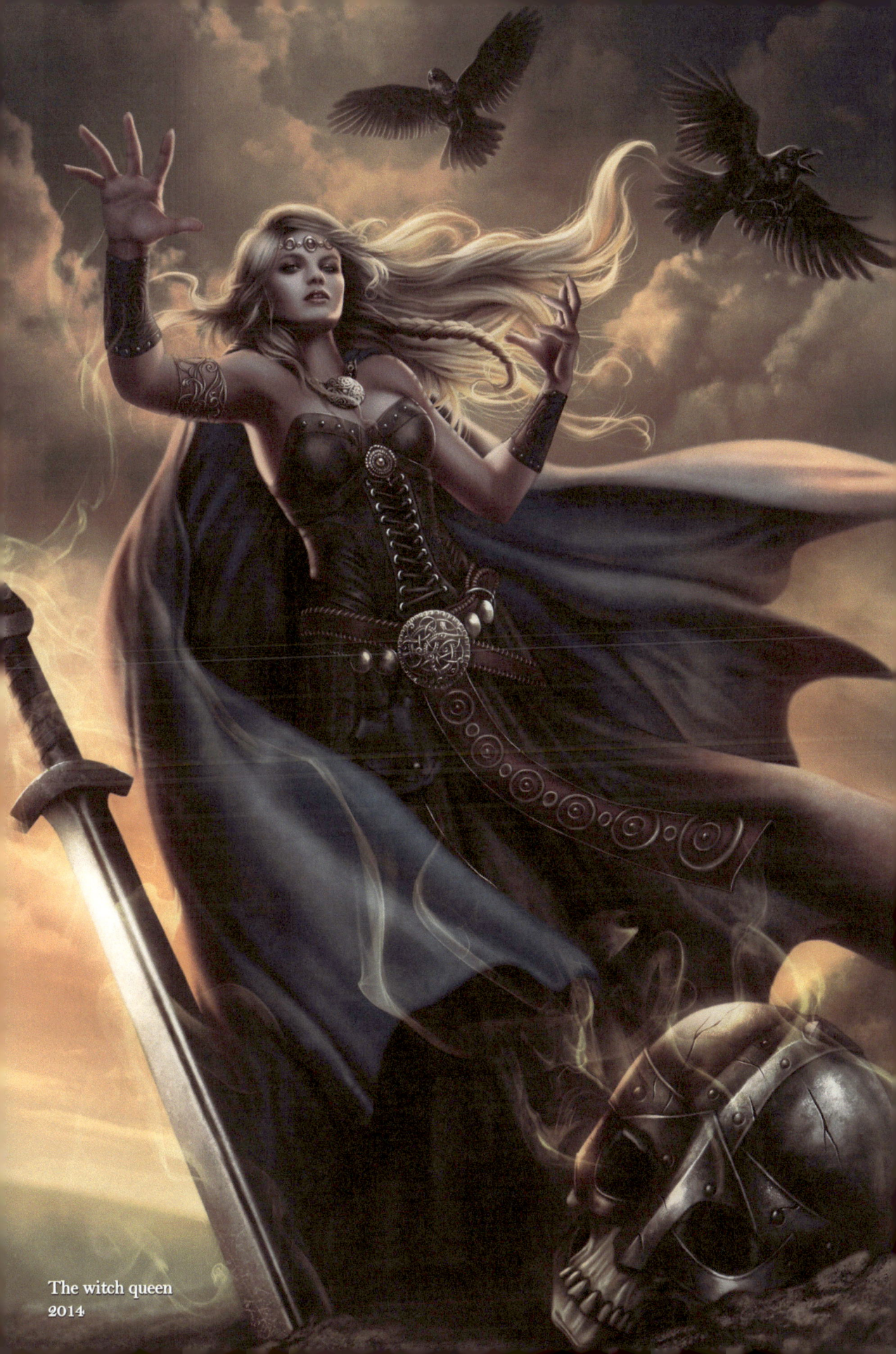

The witch queen
2014

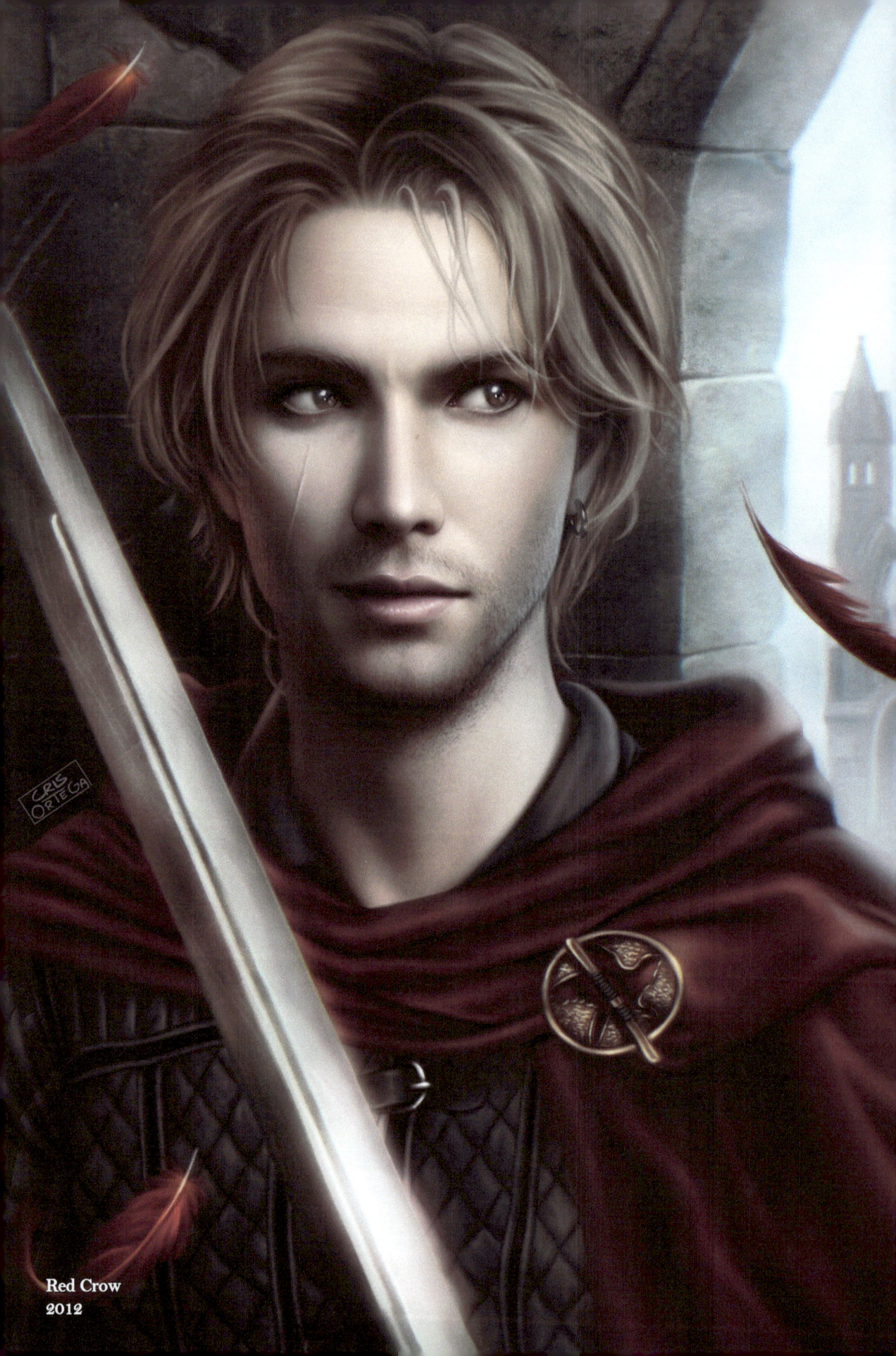

Red Crow
2012

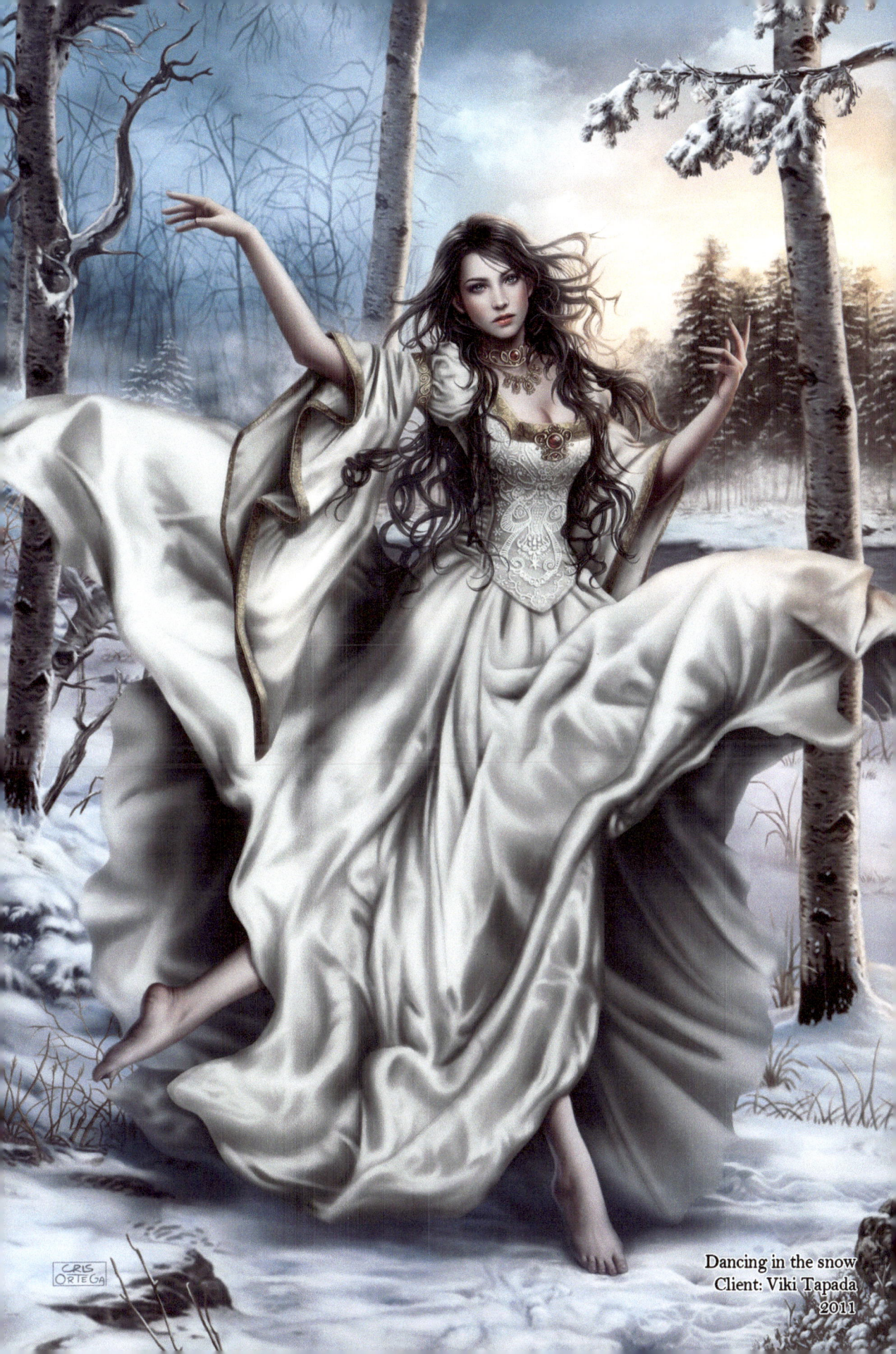

Dancing in the snow
Client: Viki Tapada
2011

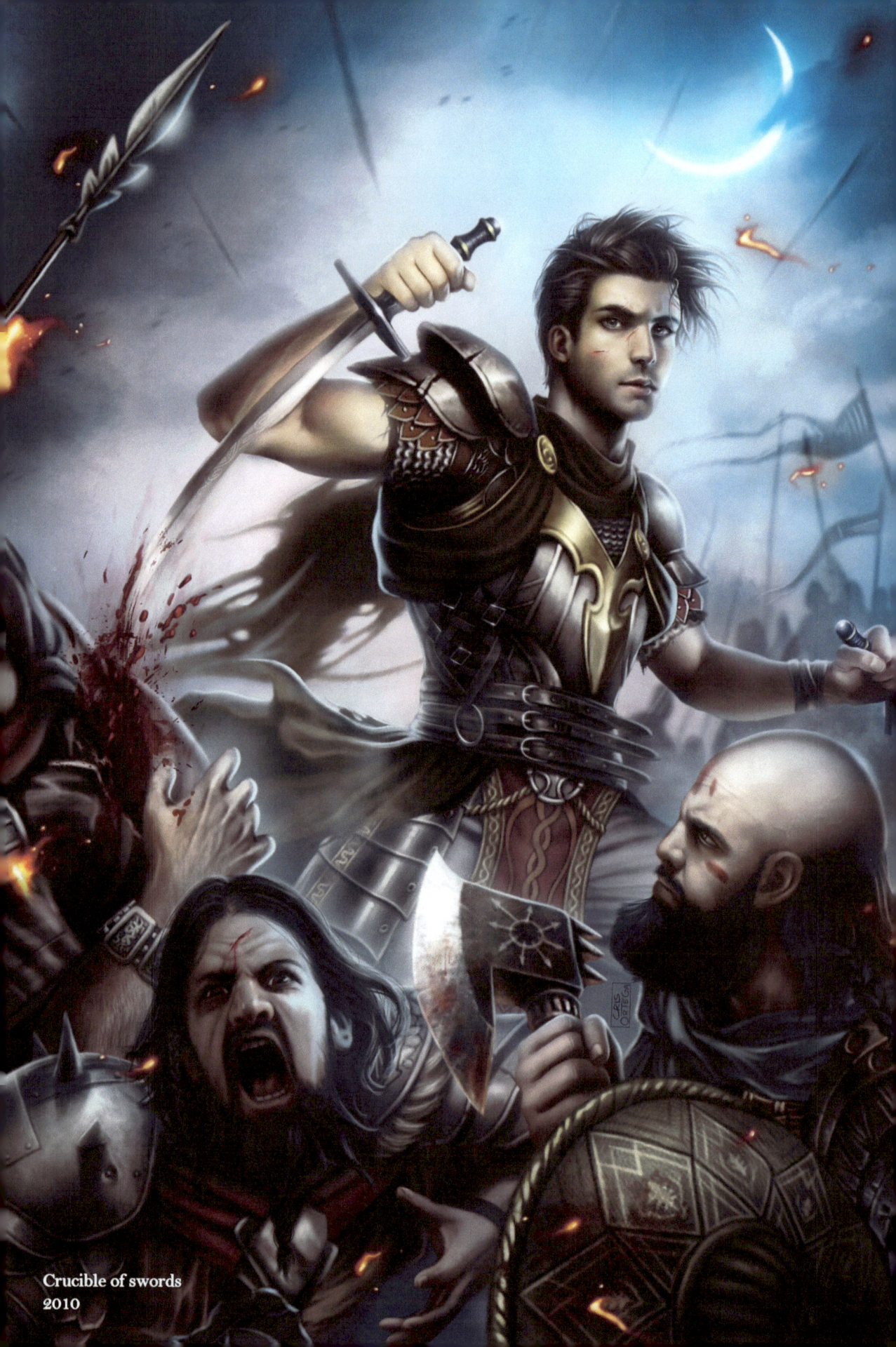

Crucible of swords
2010

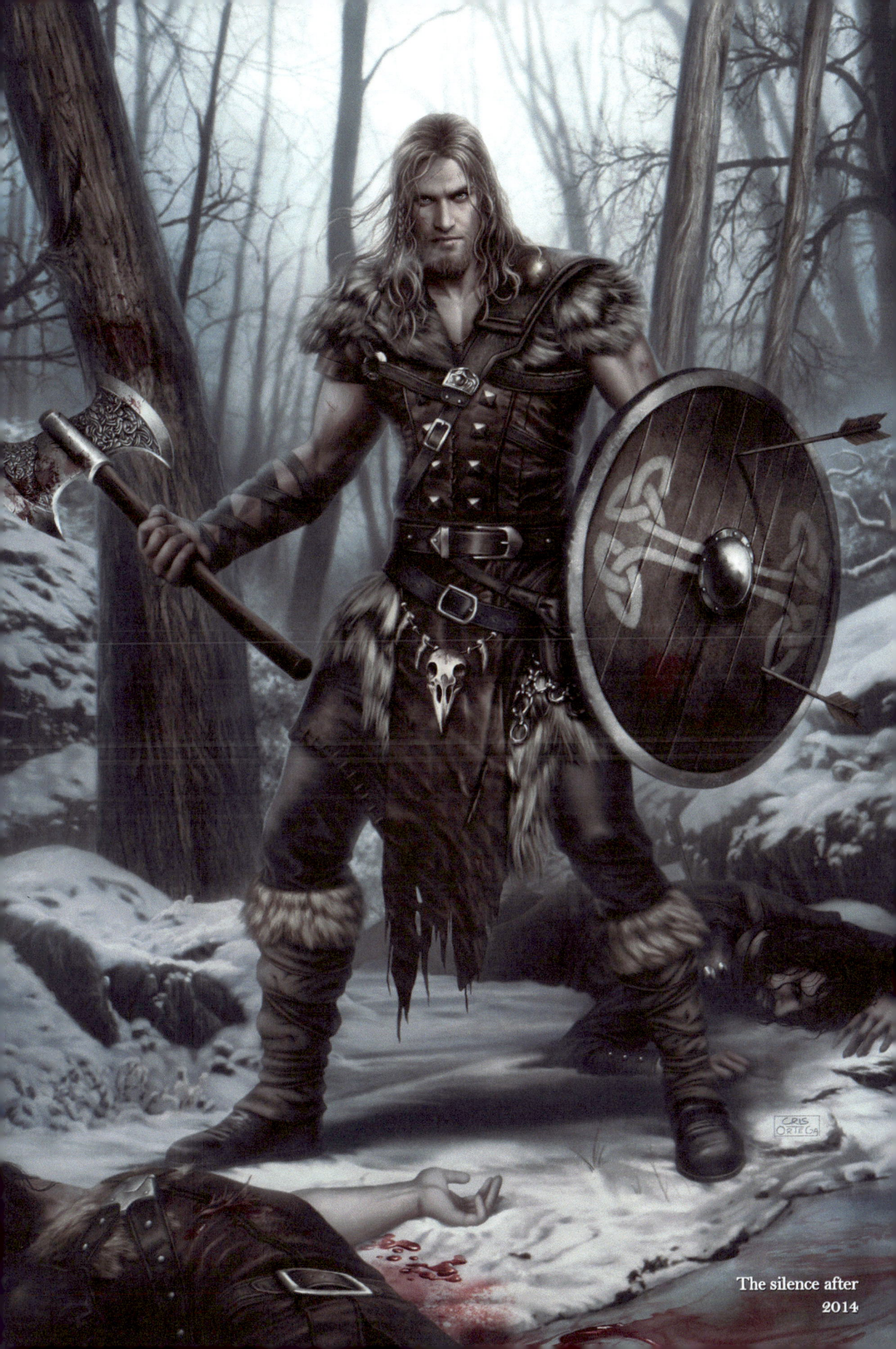

The silence after
2014

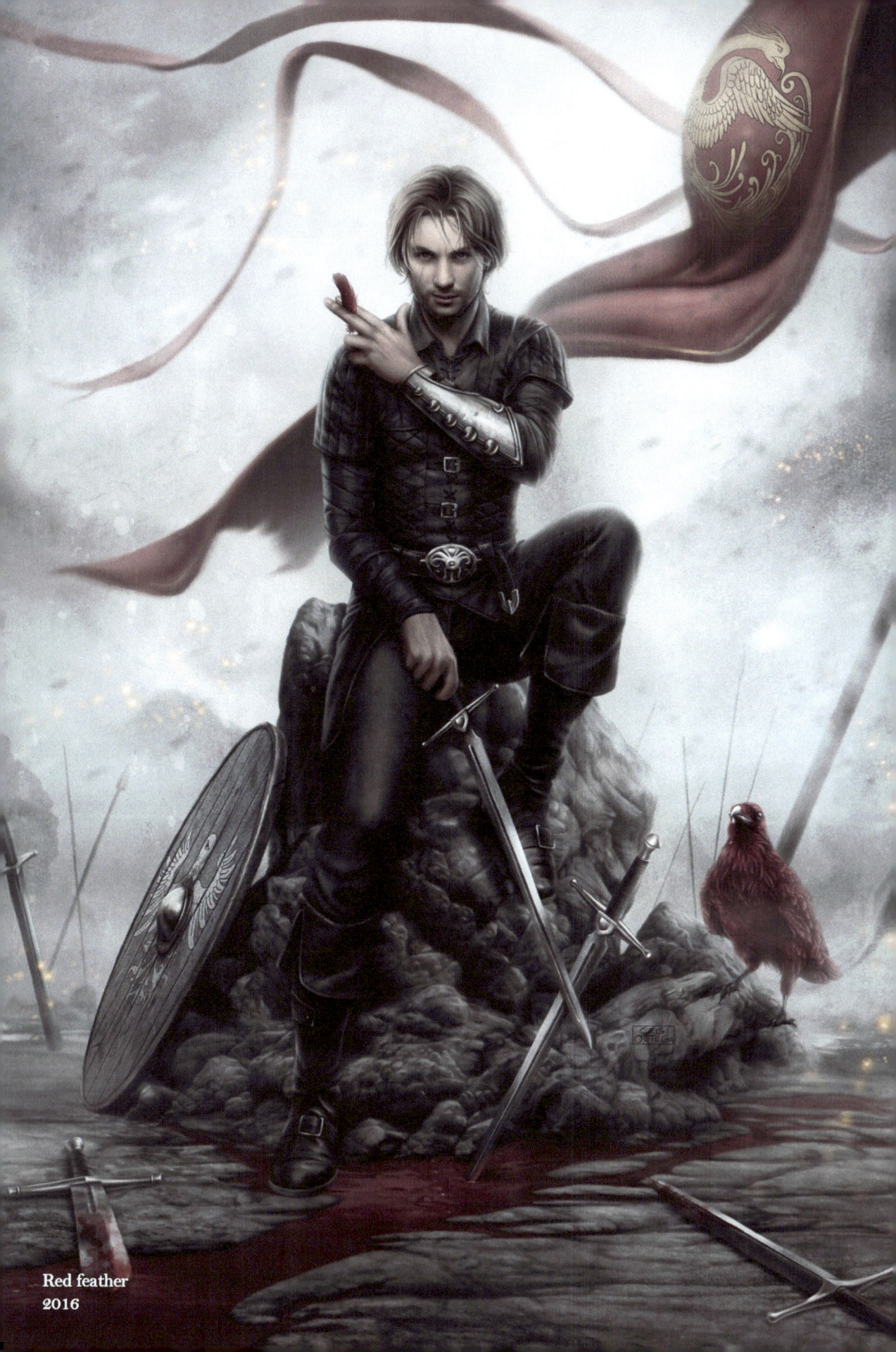

Red feather
2016

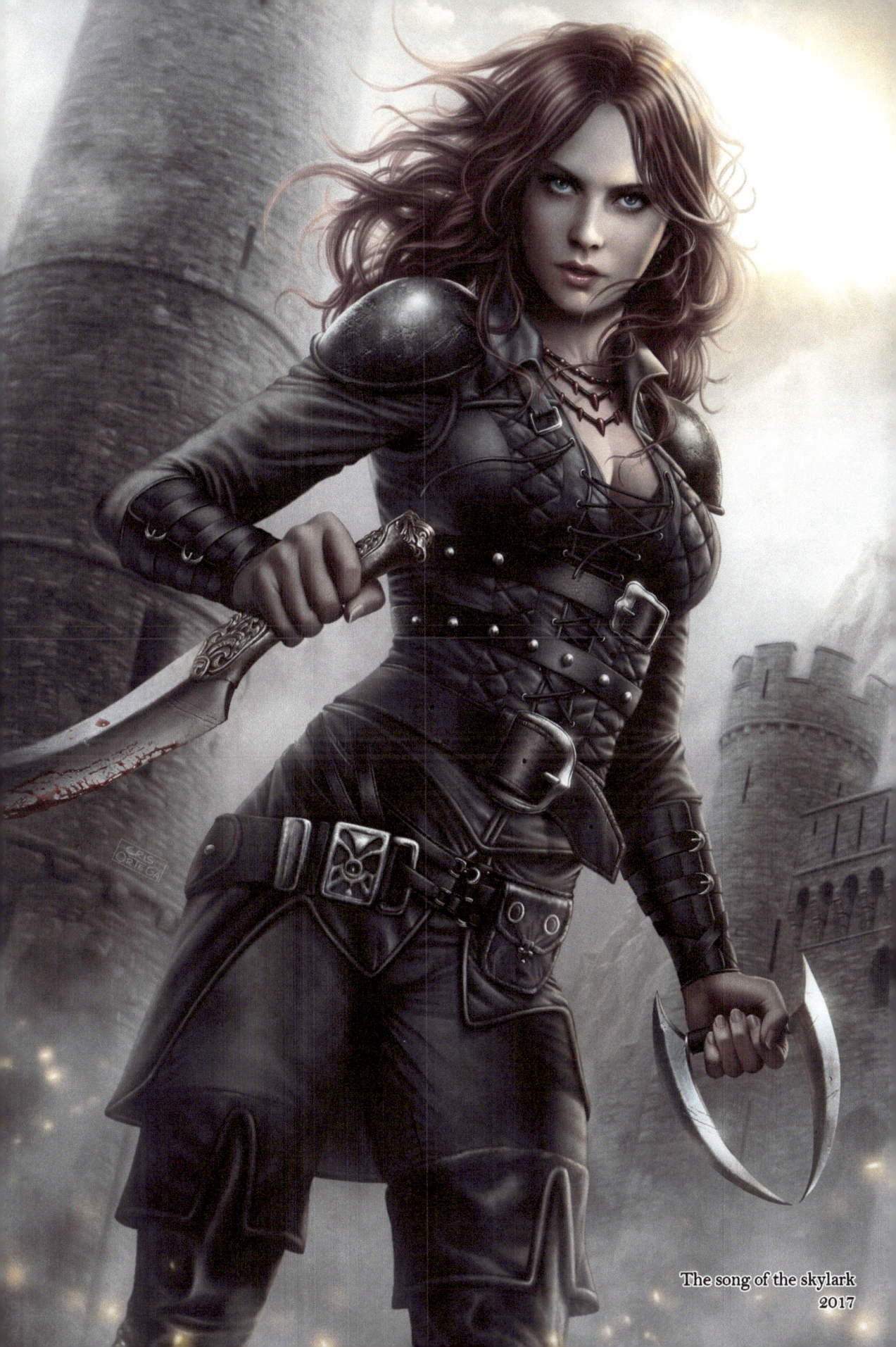

The song of the skylark
2017

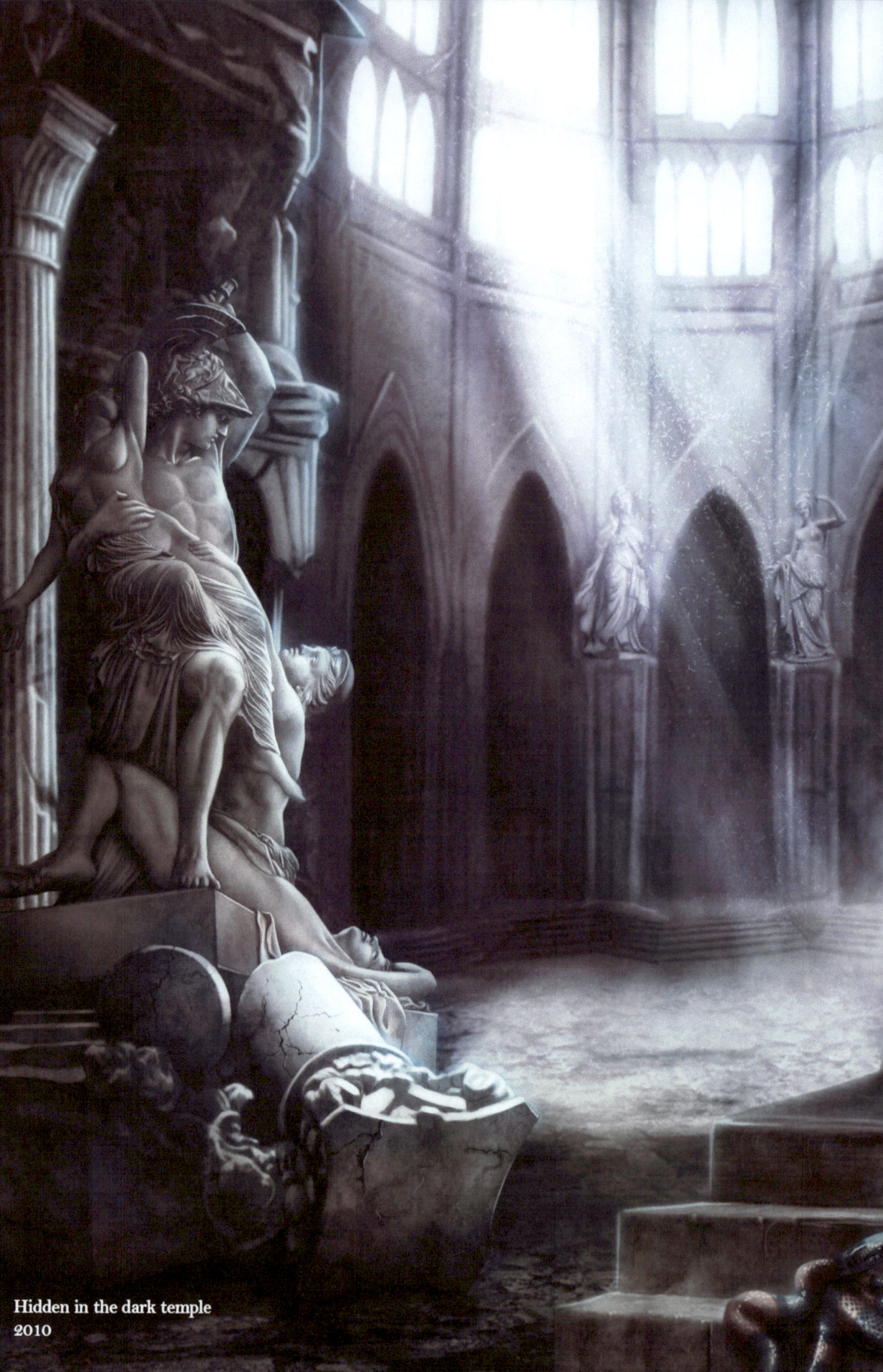

Hidden in the dark temple
2010

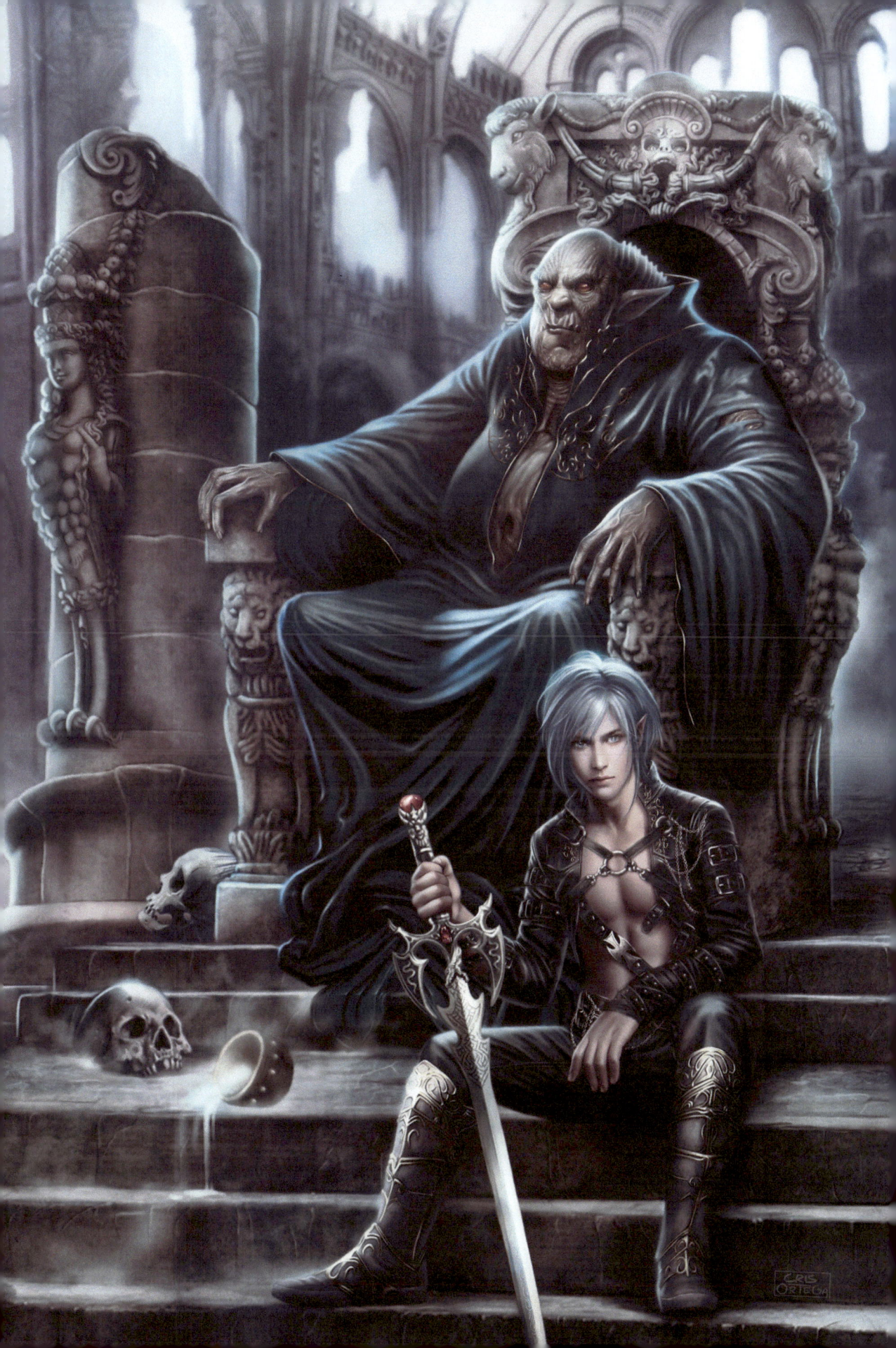

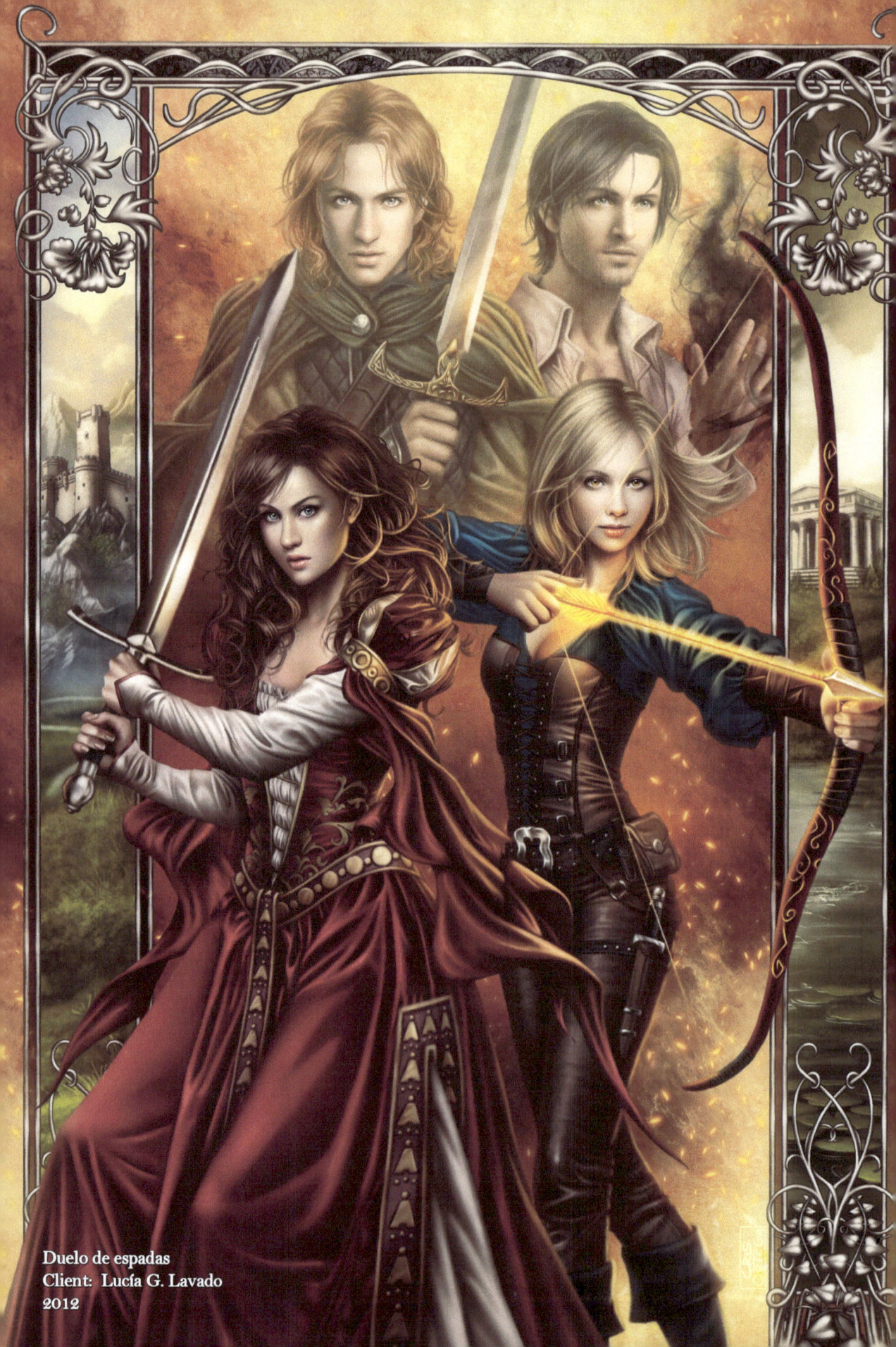

Duelo de espadas
Client: Lucía G. Lavado
2012

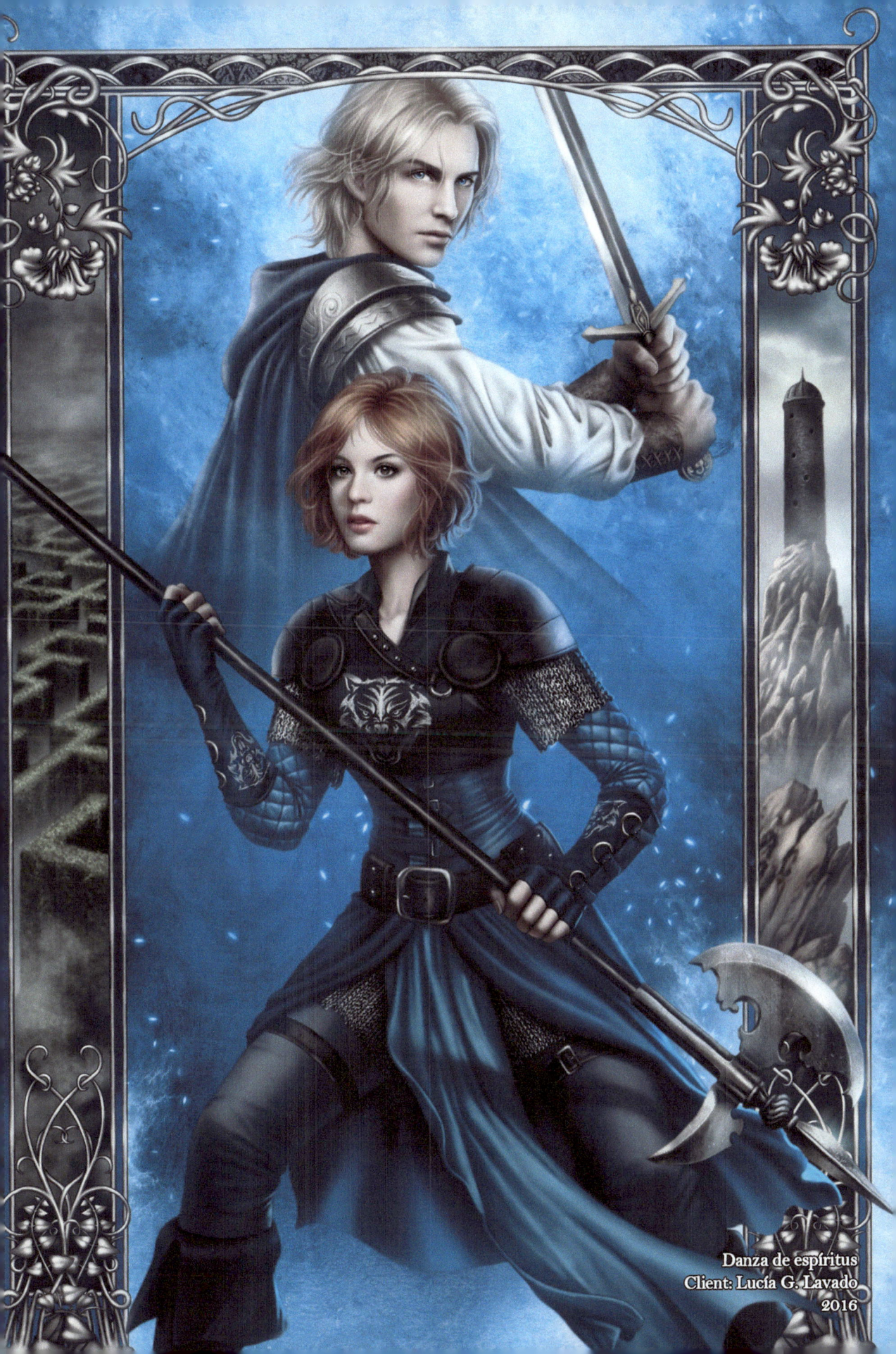

Danza de espíritus
Client: Lucía G. Lavado
2016

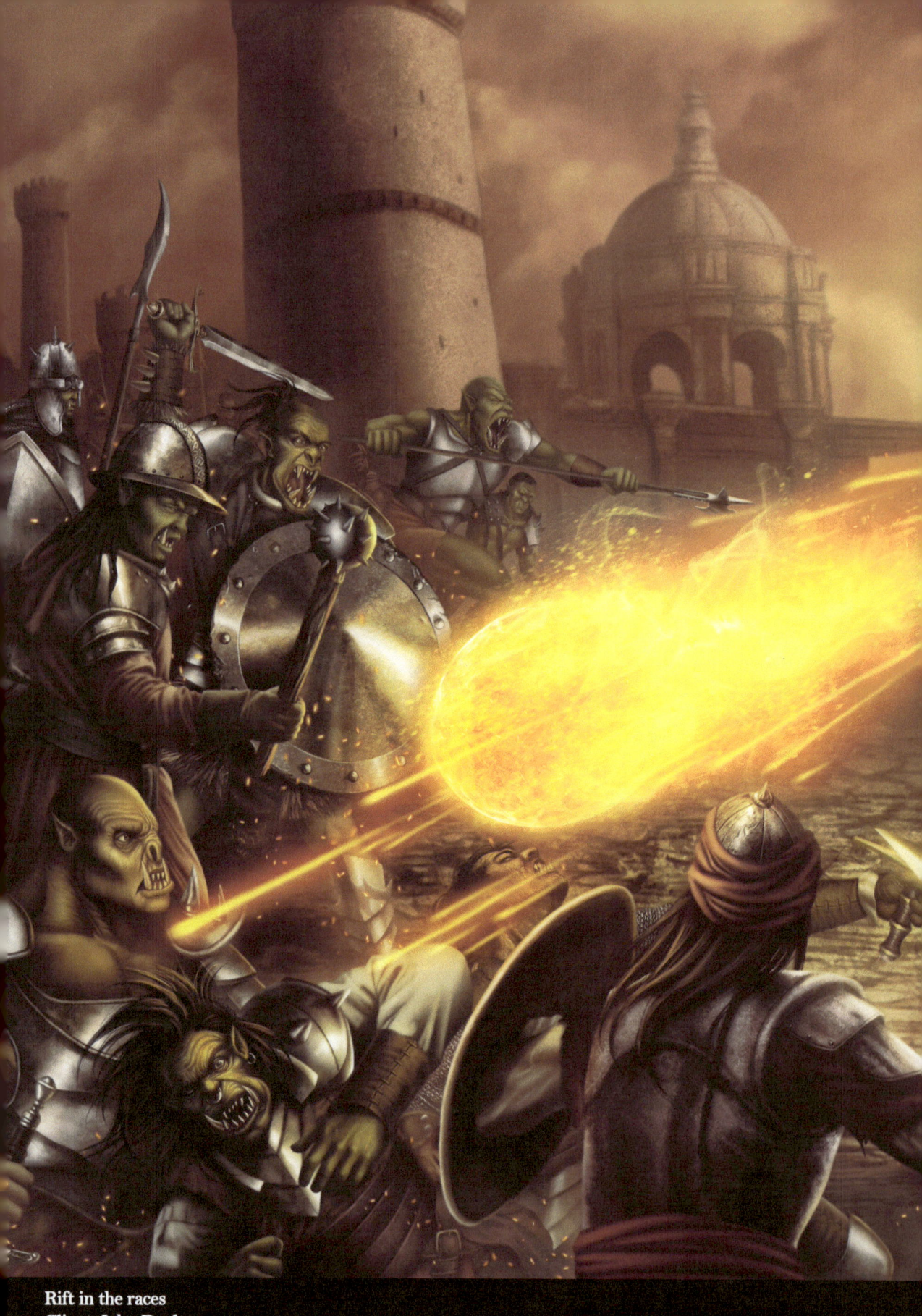

Rift in the races
Client: John Daulton
2012

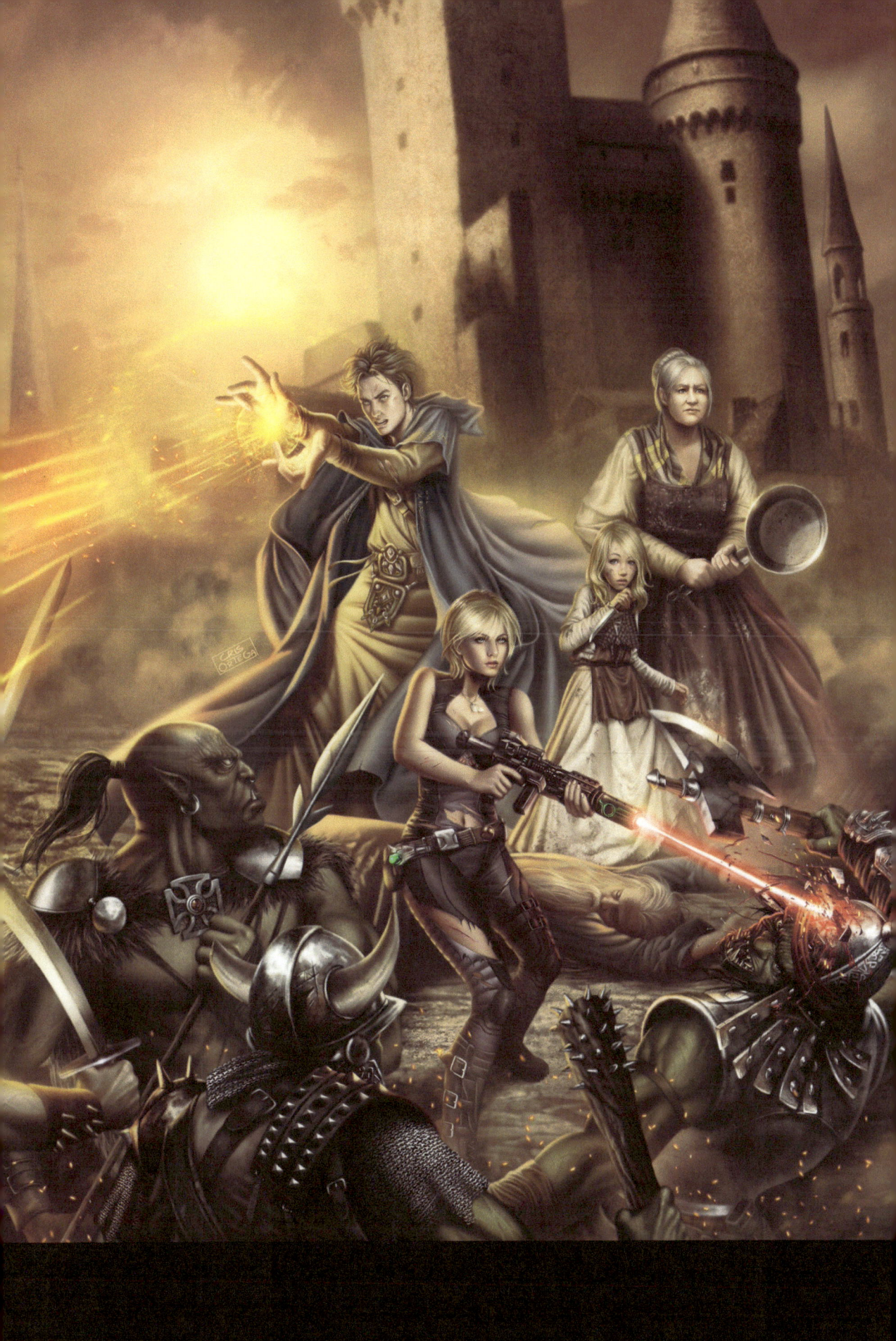

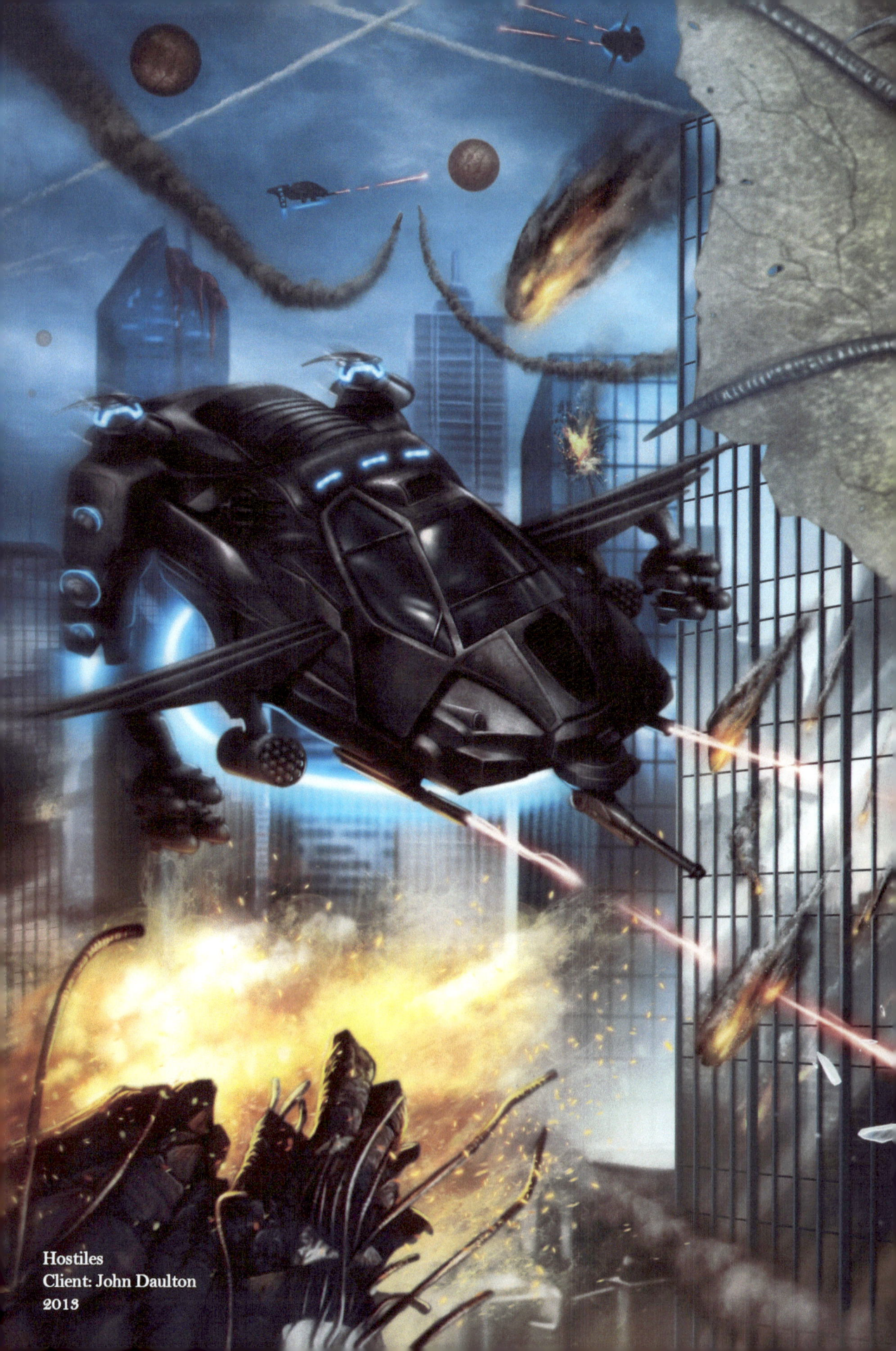

Hostiles
Client: John Daulton
2013

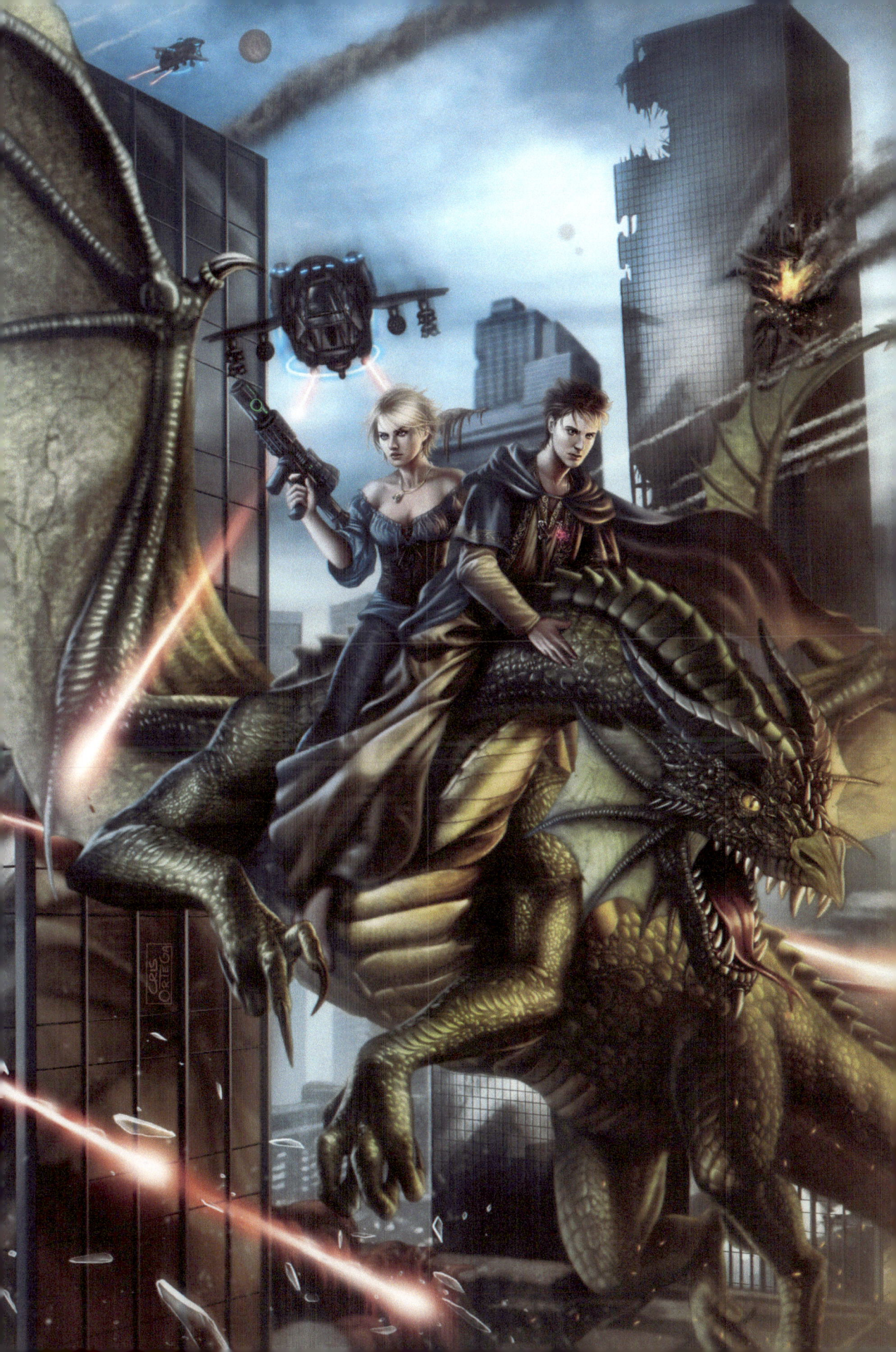

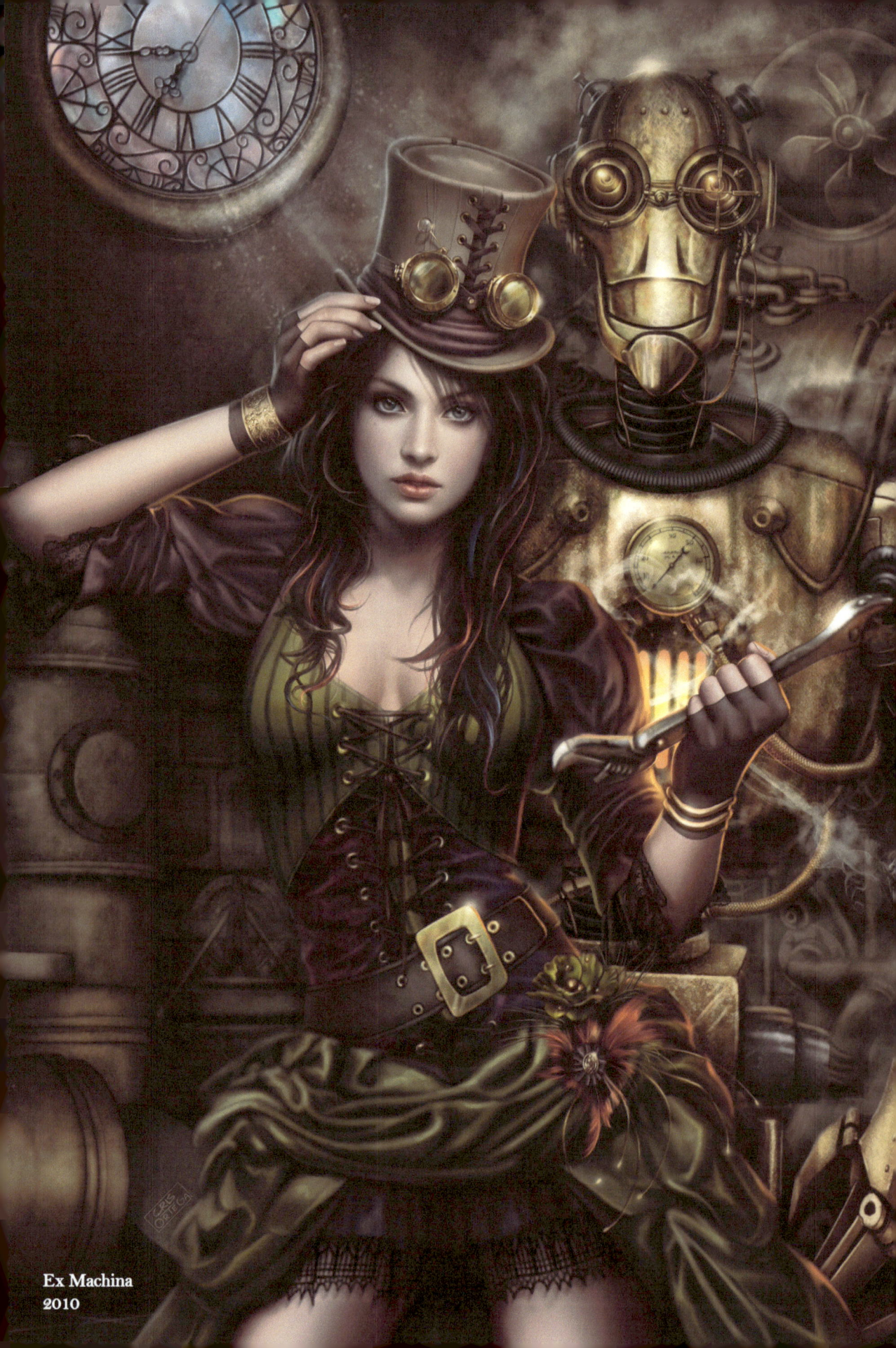

Ex Machina
2010

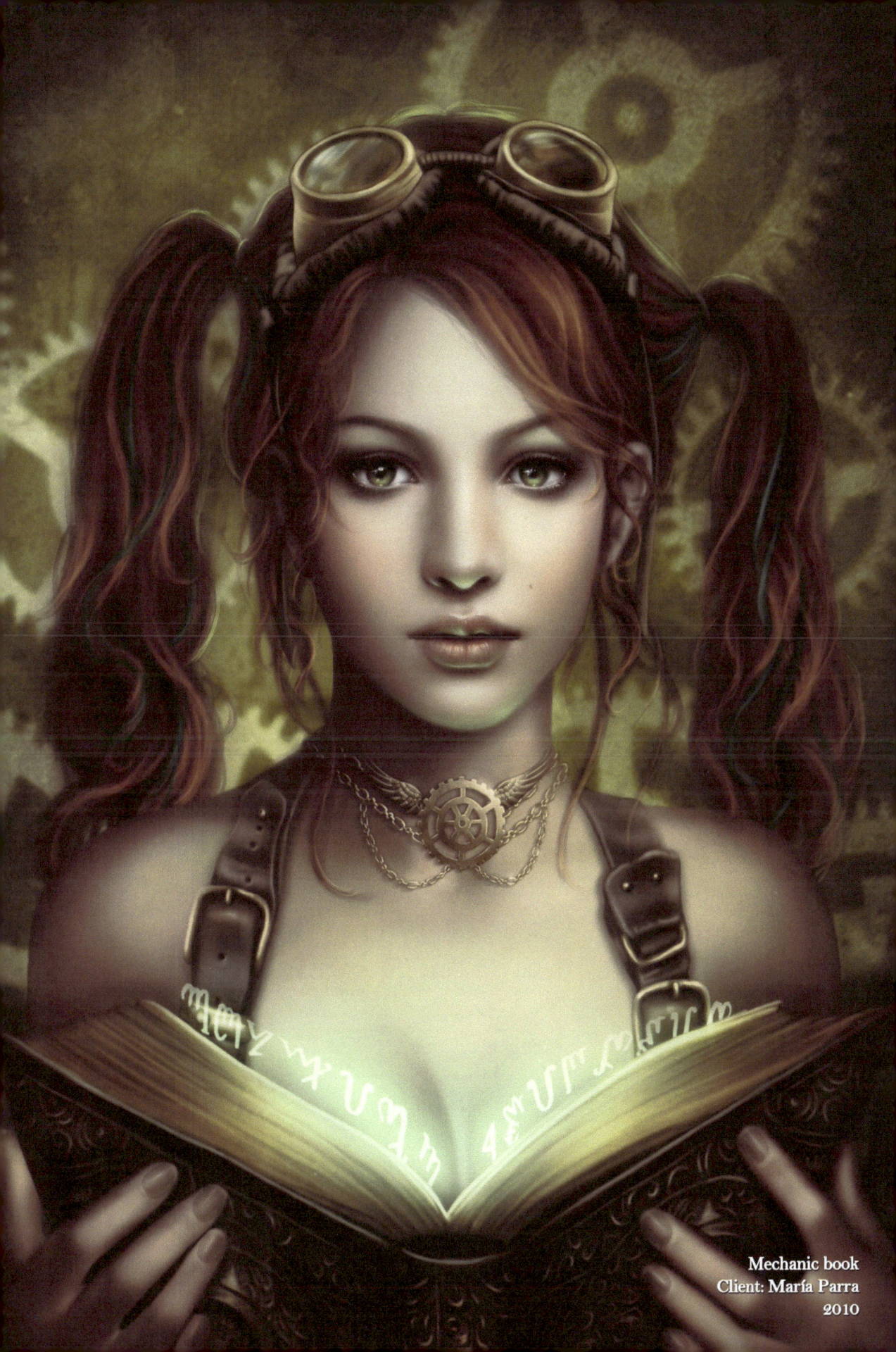

Mechanic book
Client: María Parra
2010

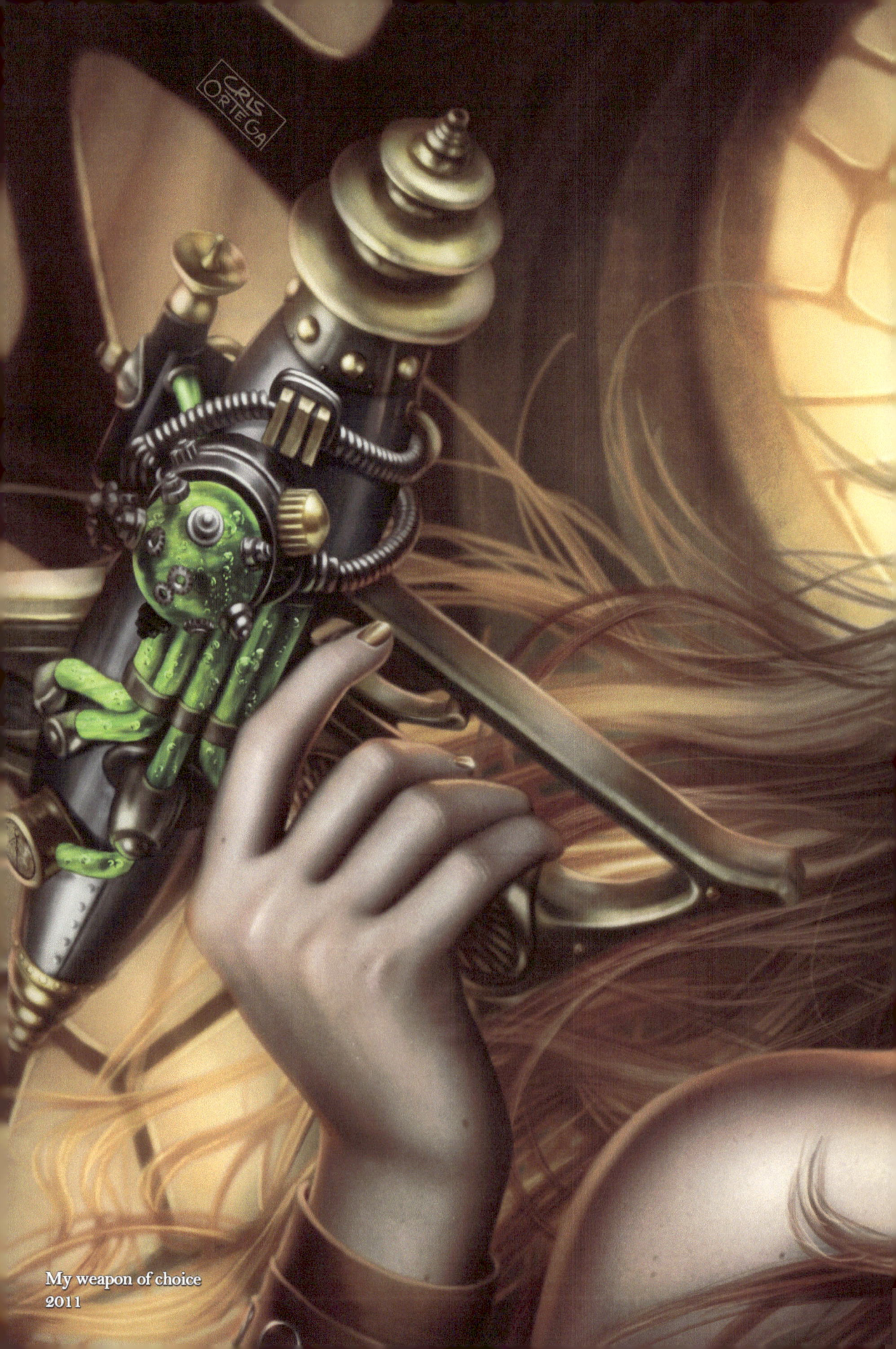

My weapon of choice
2011

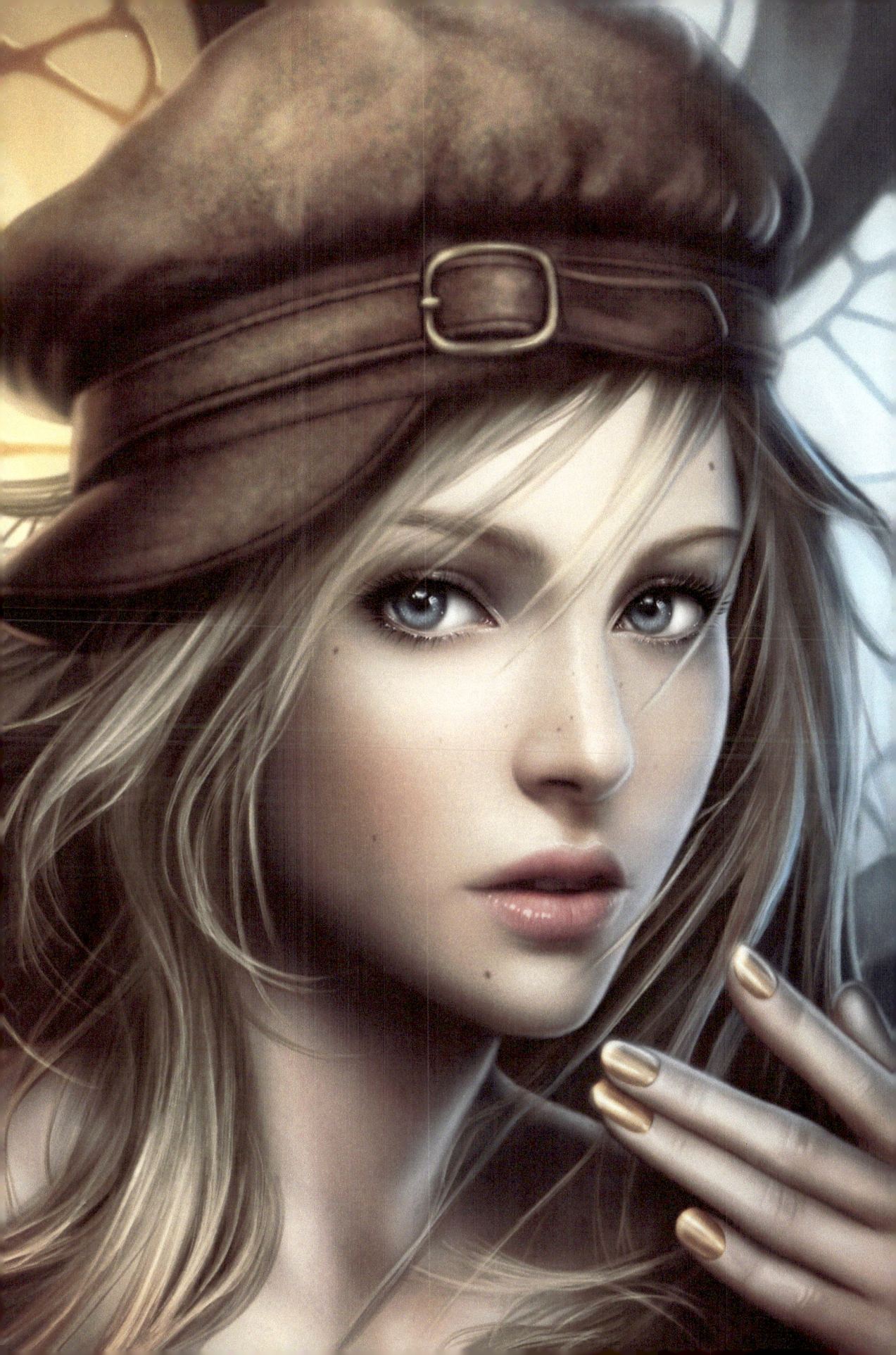

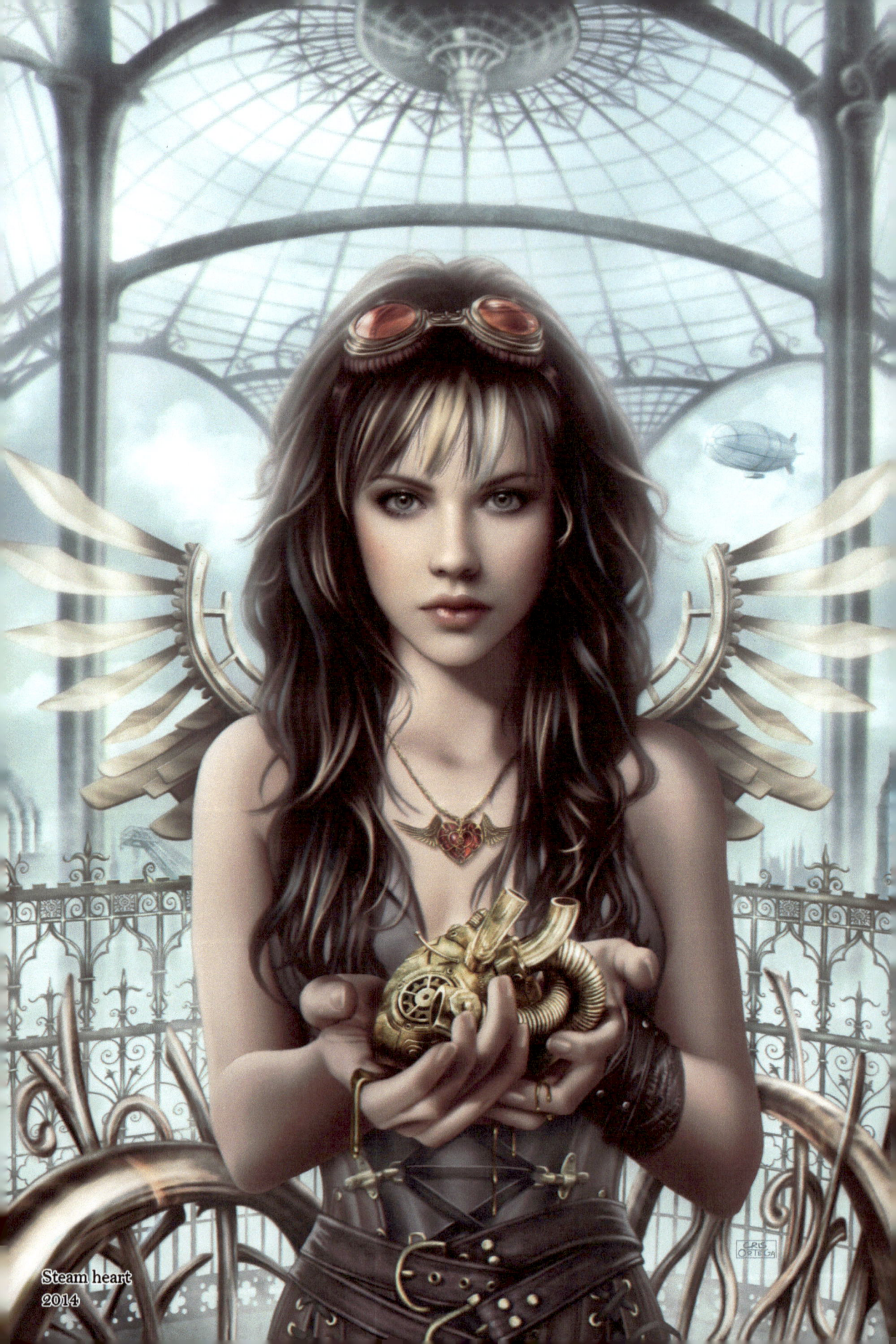

Steam heart
2014

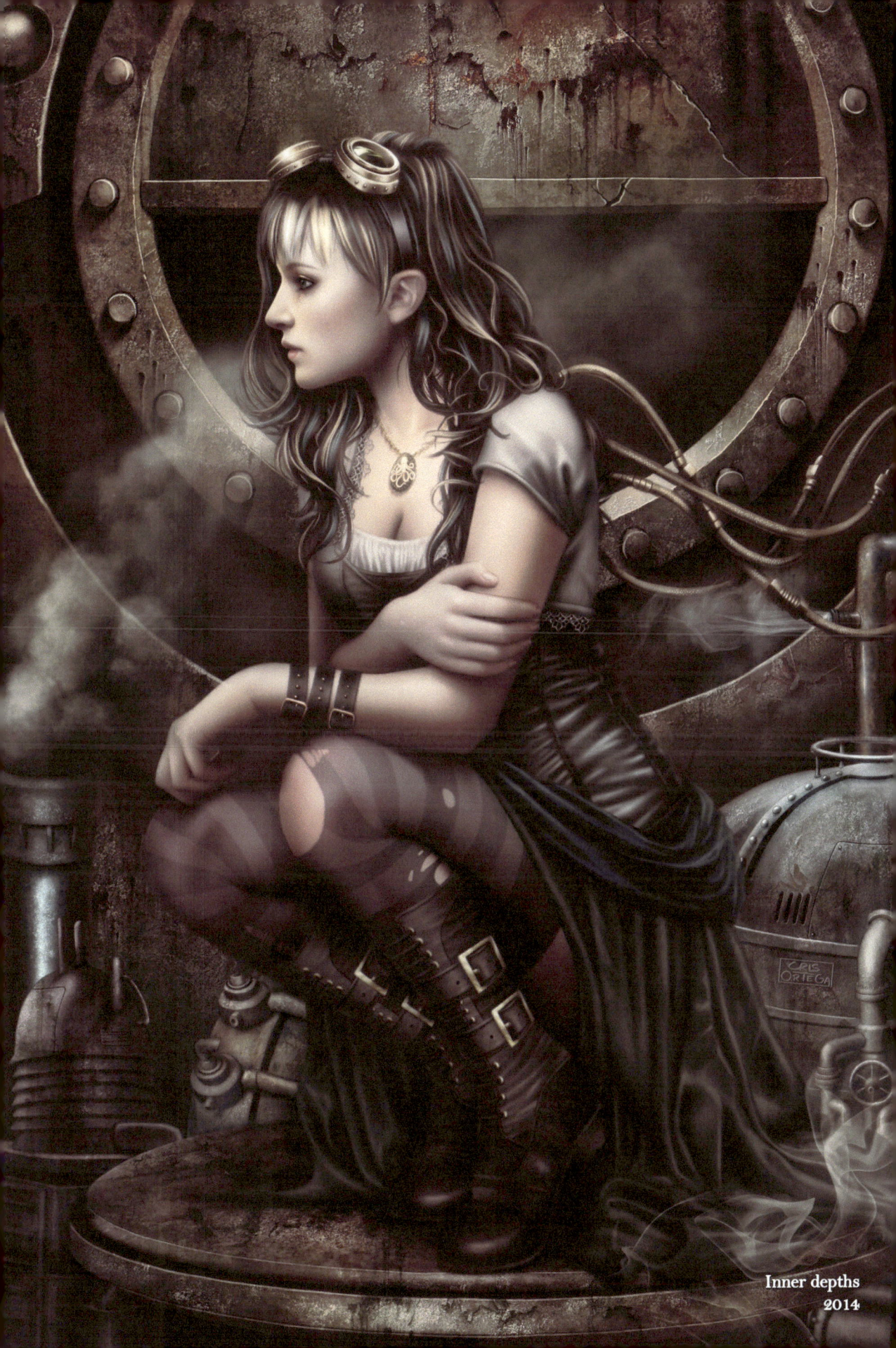

Inner depths
2014

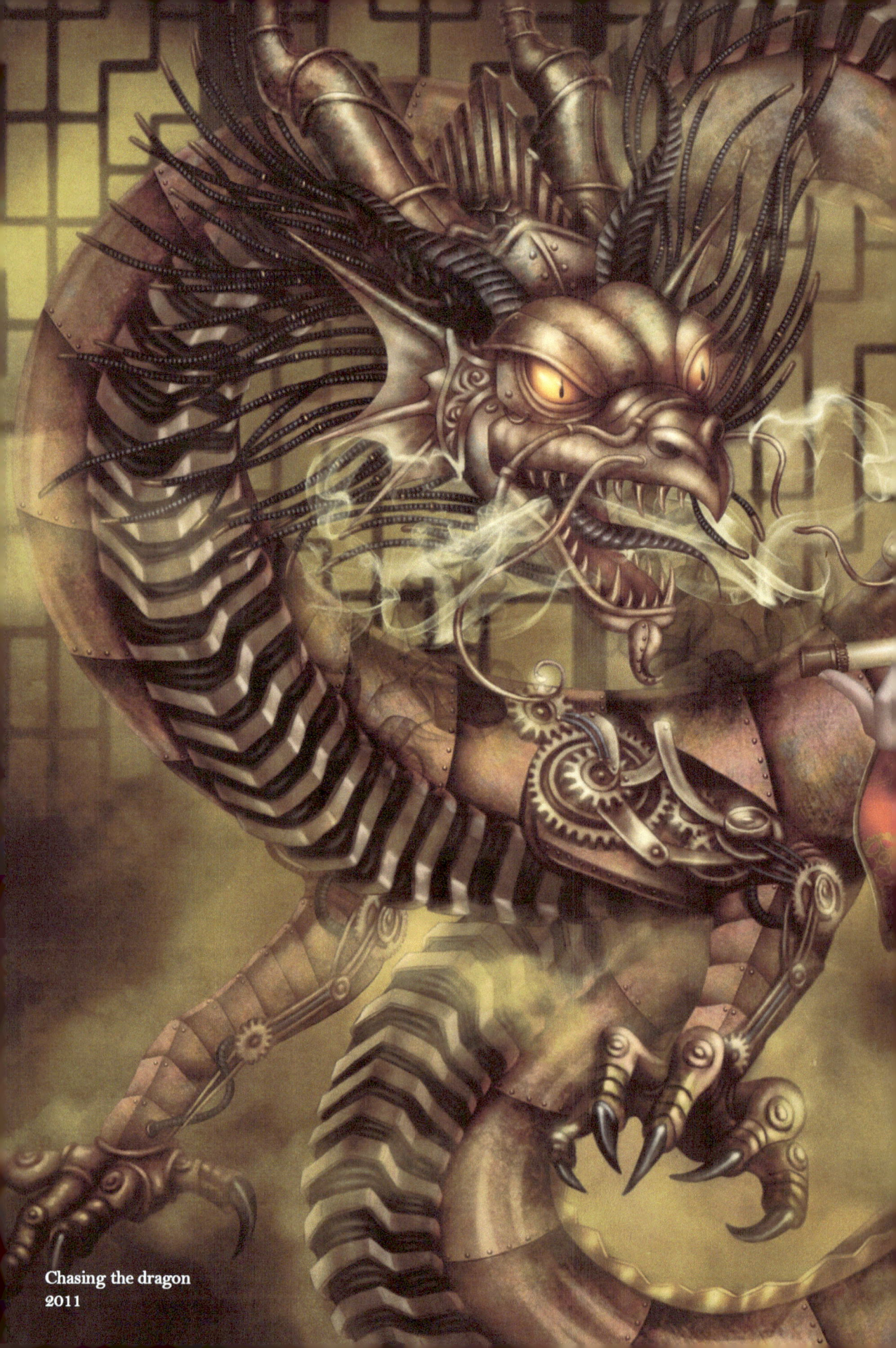

Chasing the dragon
2011

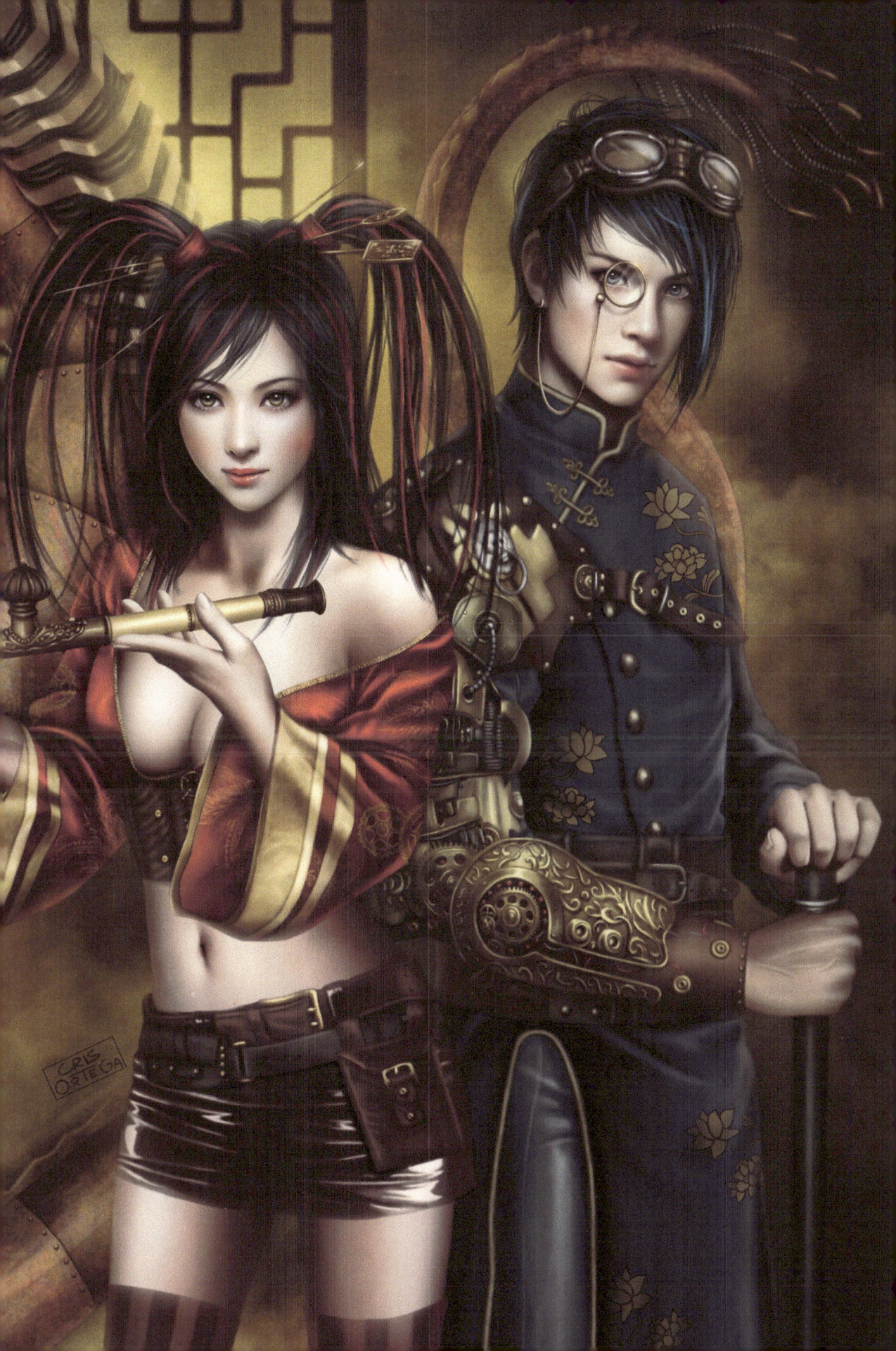

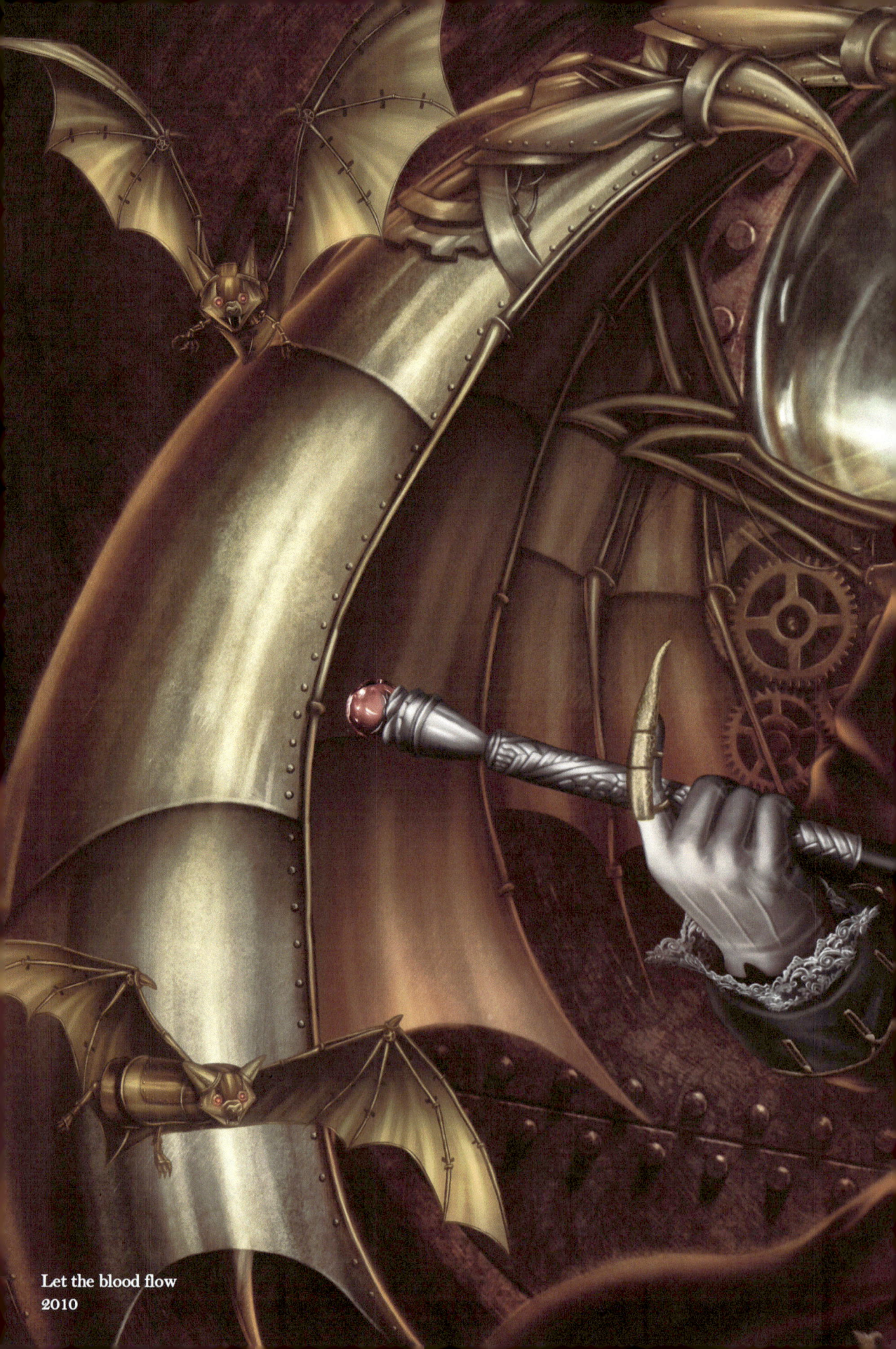

Let the blood flow
2010

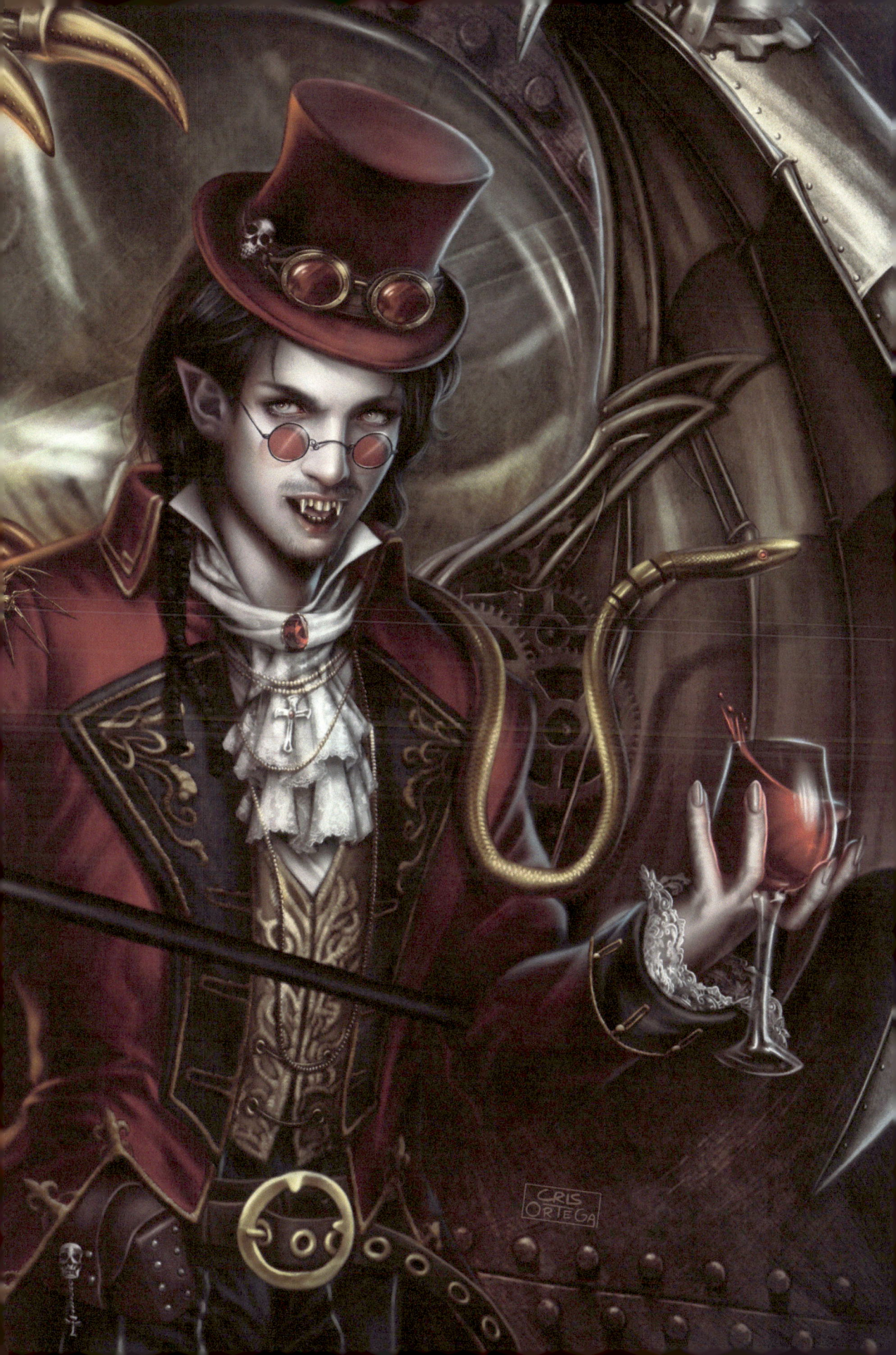

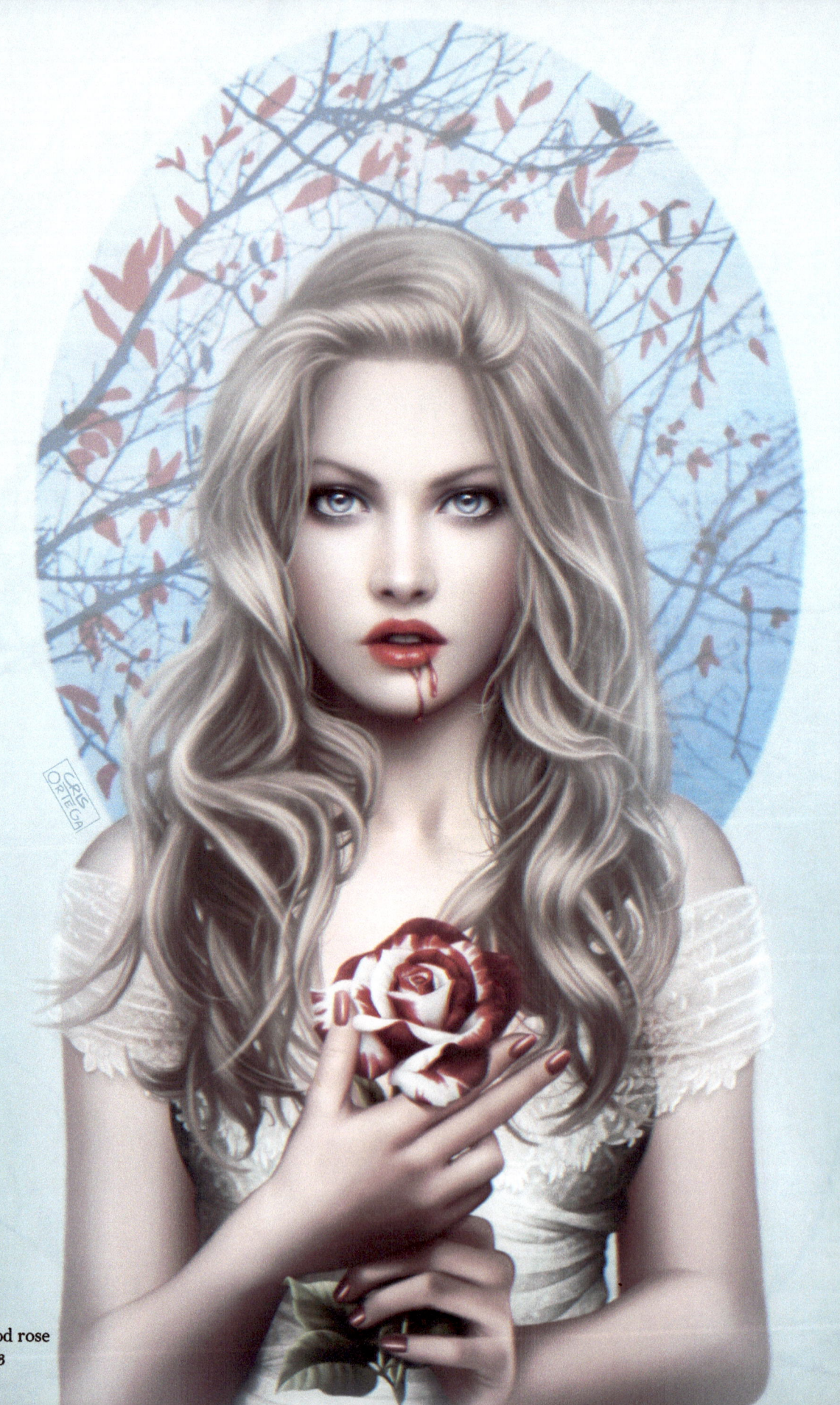

CRIS
ORTEGA

Blood rose
2013

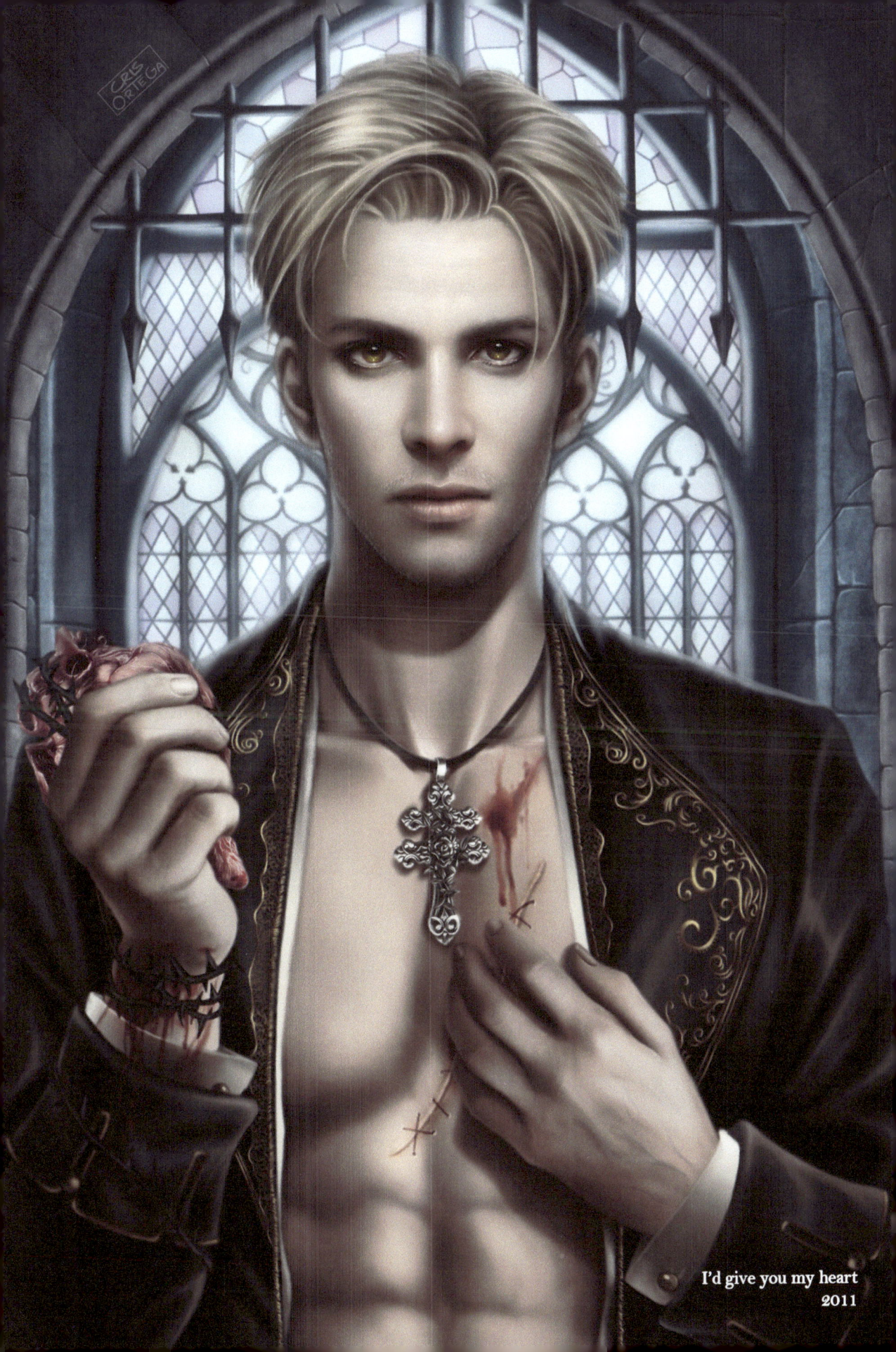

I'd give you my heart
2011

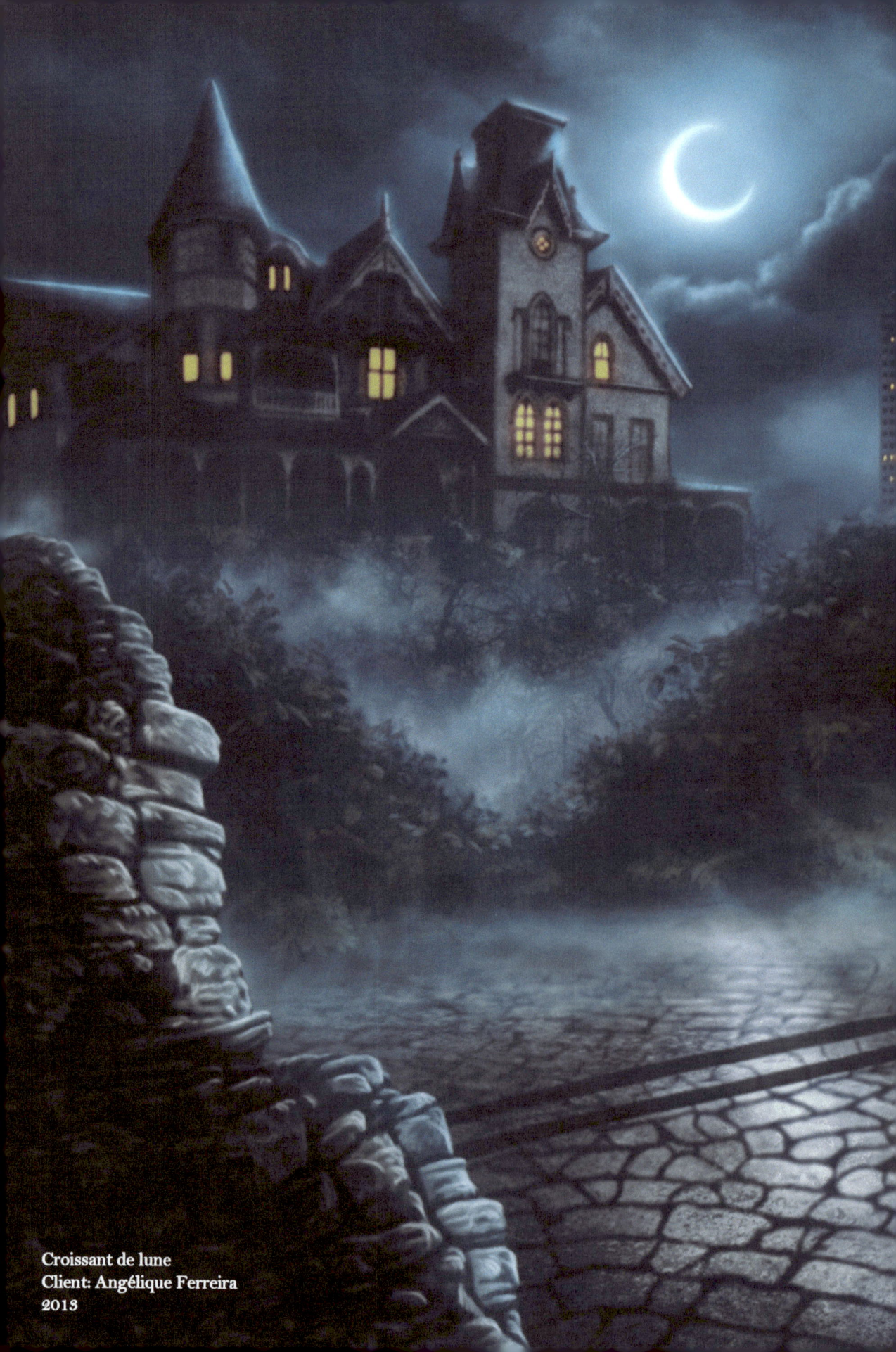

Croissant de lune
Client: Angélique Ferreira
2013

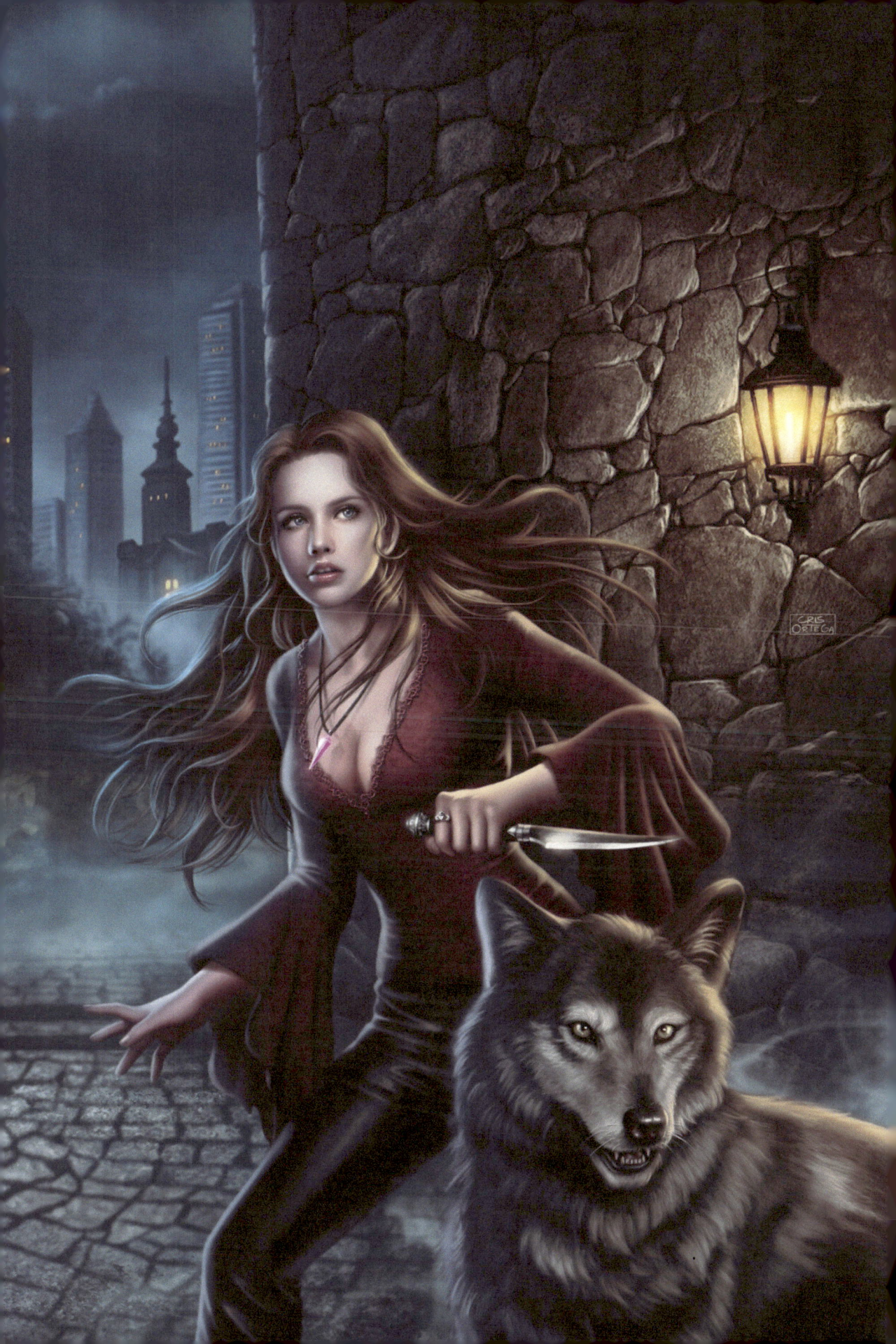

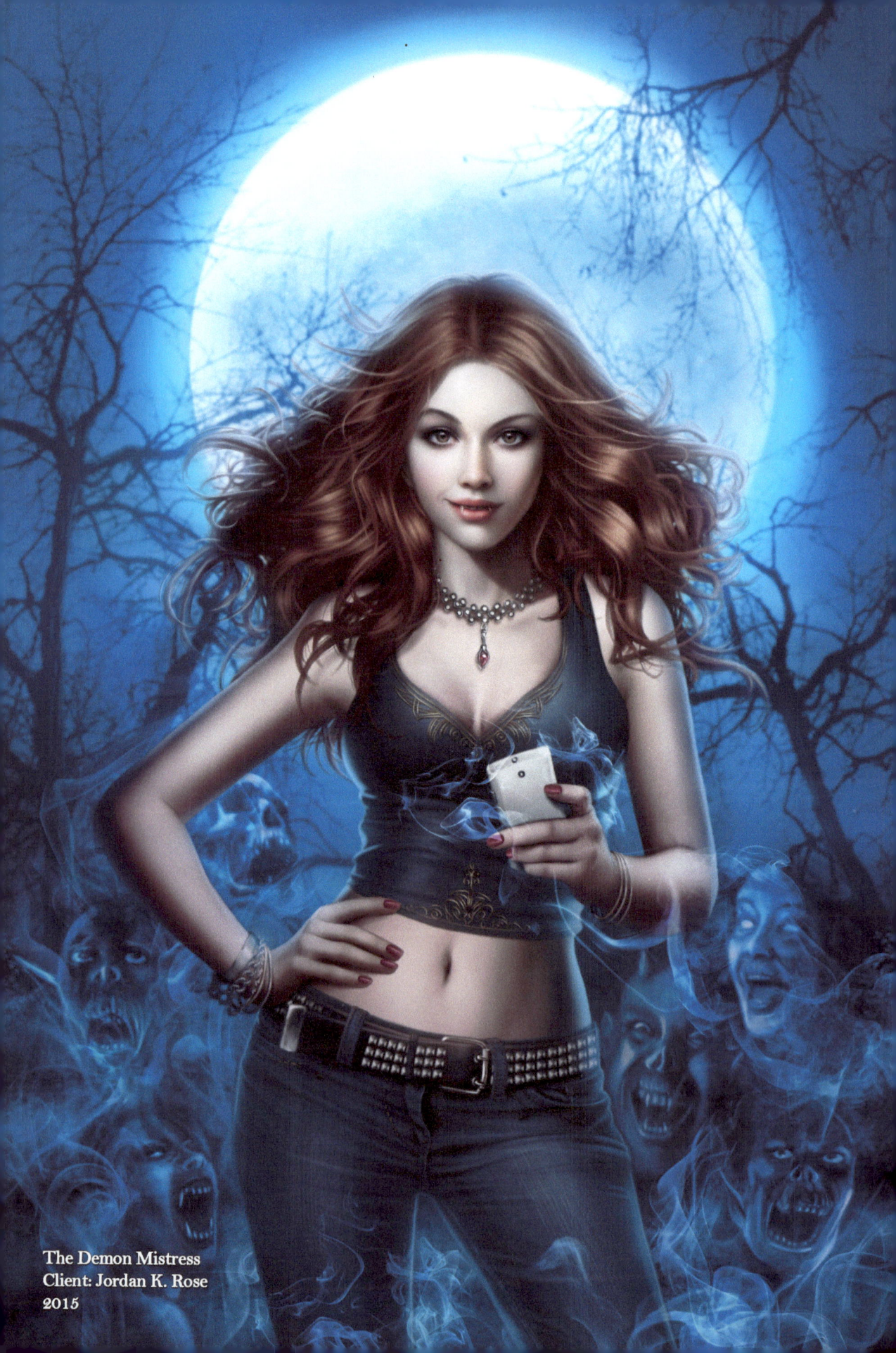

The Demon Mistress
Client: Jordan K. Rose
2015

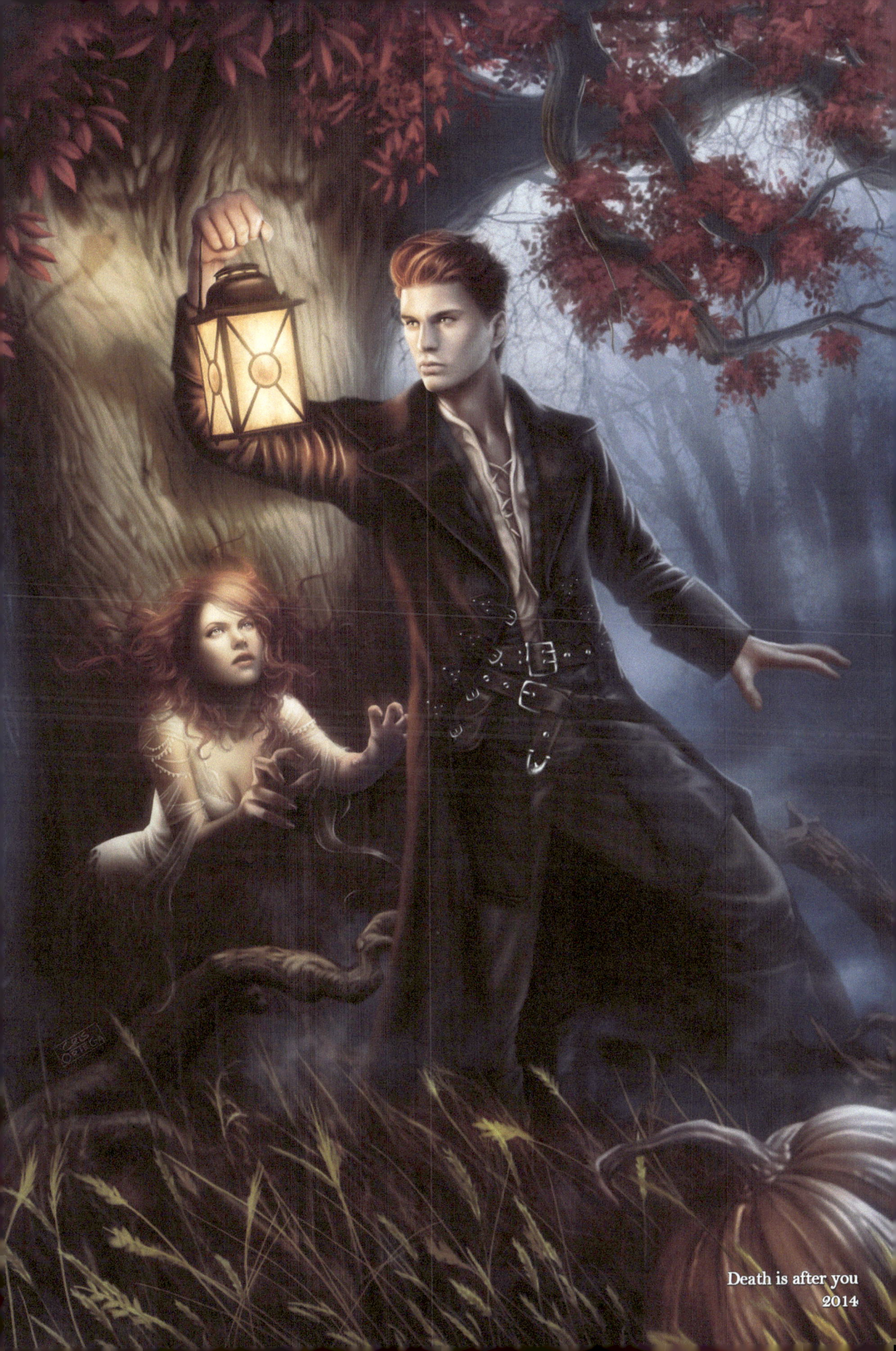

Death is after you
2014

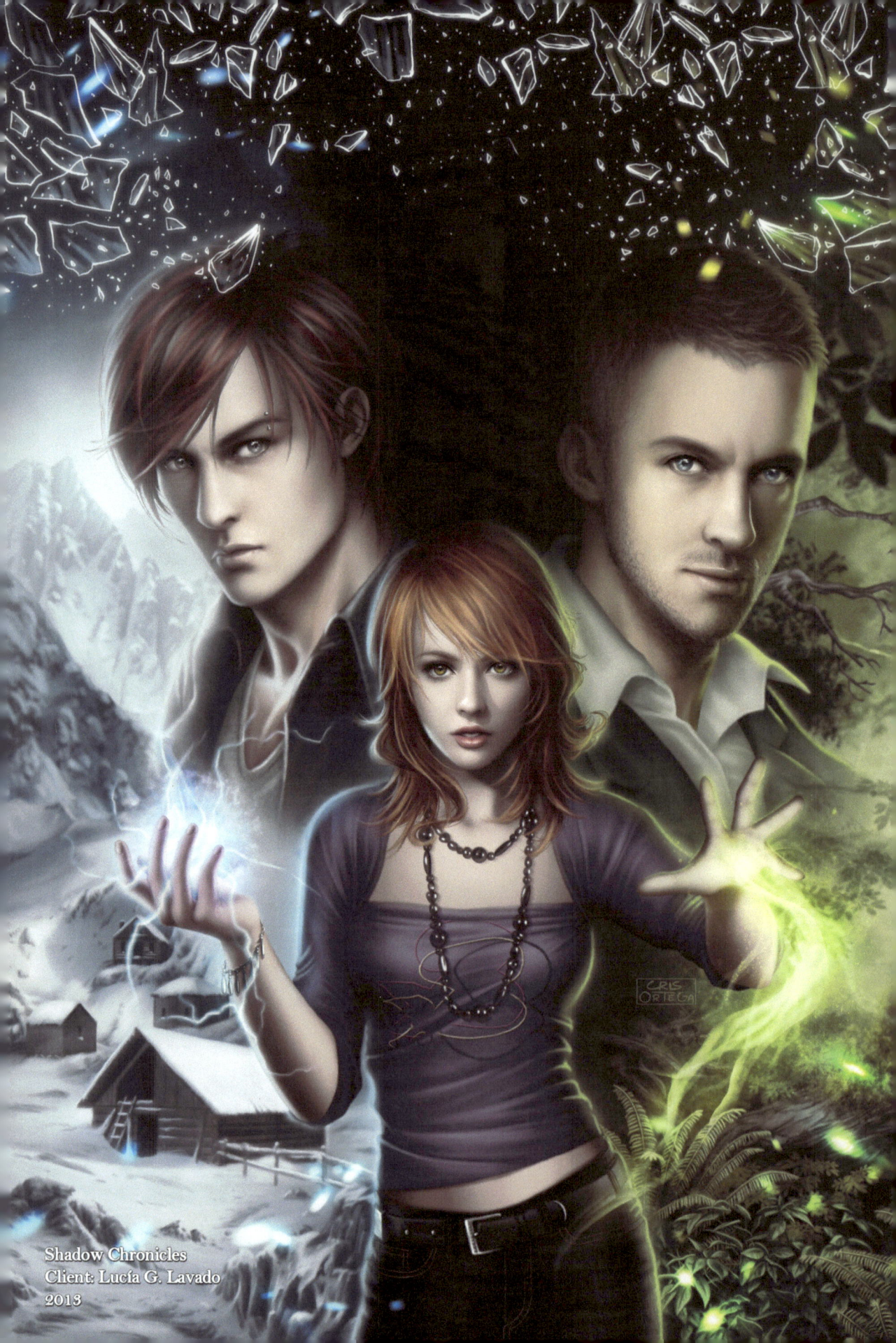

Shadow Chronicles
Client: Lucía G. Lavado
2013

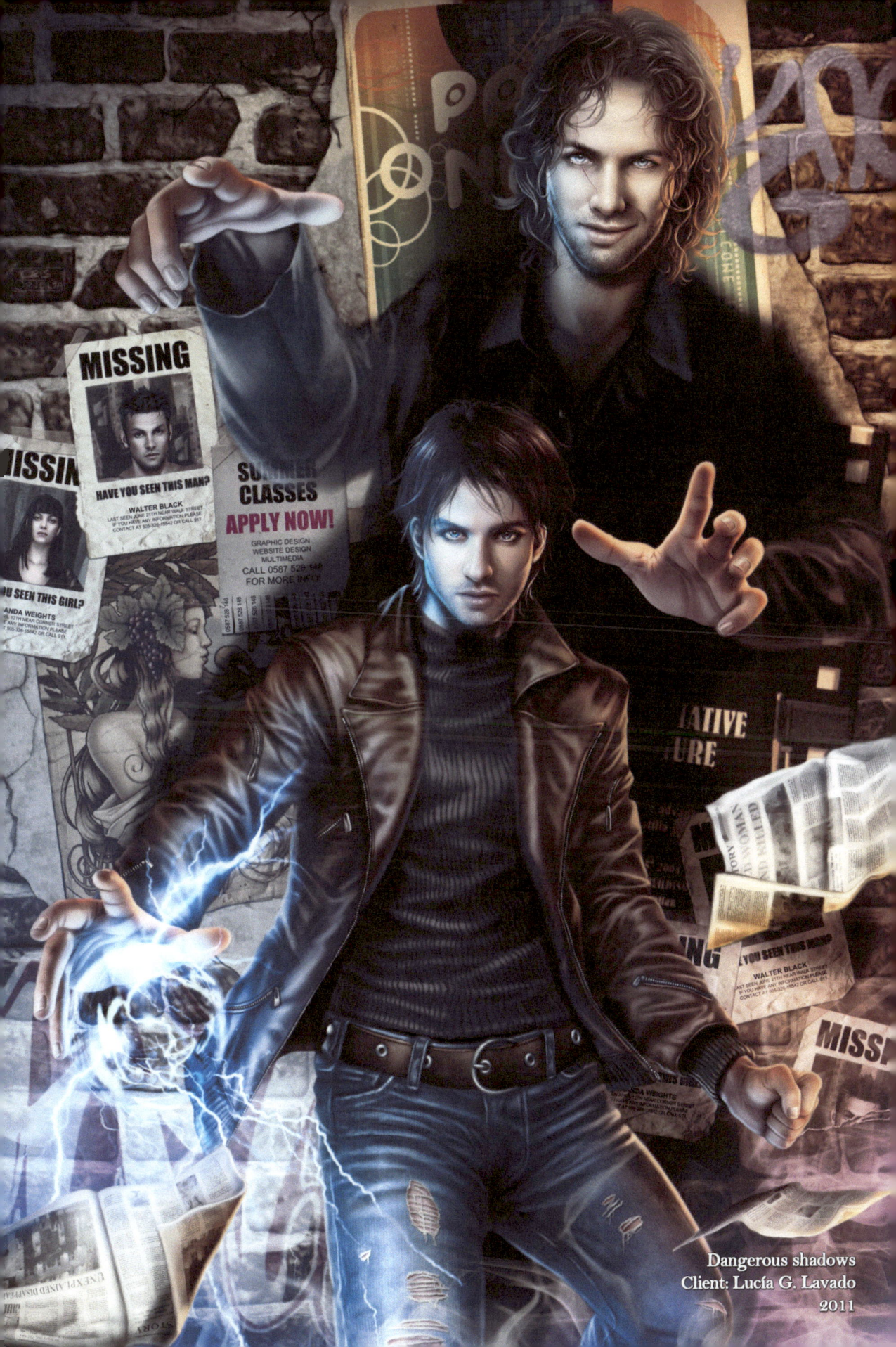

Dangerous shadows
Client: Lucía G. Lavado
2011

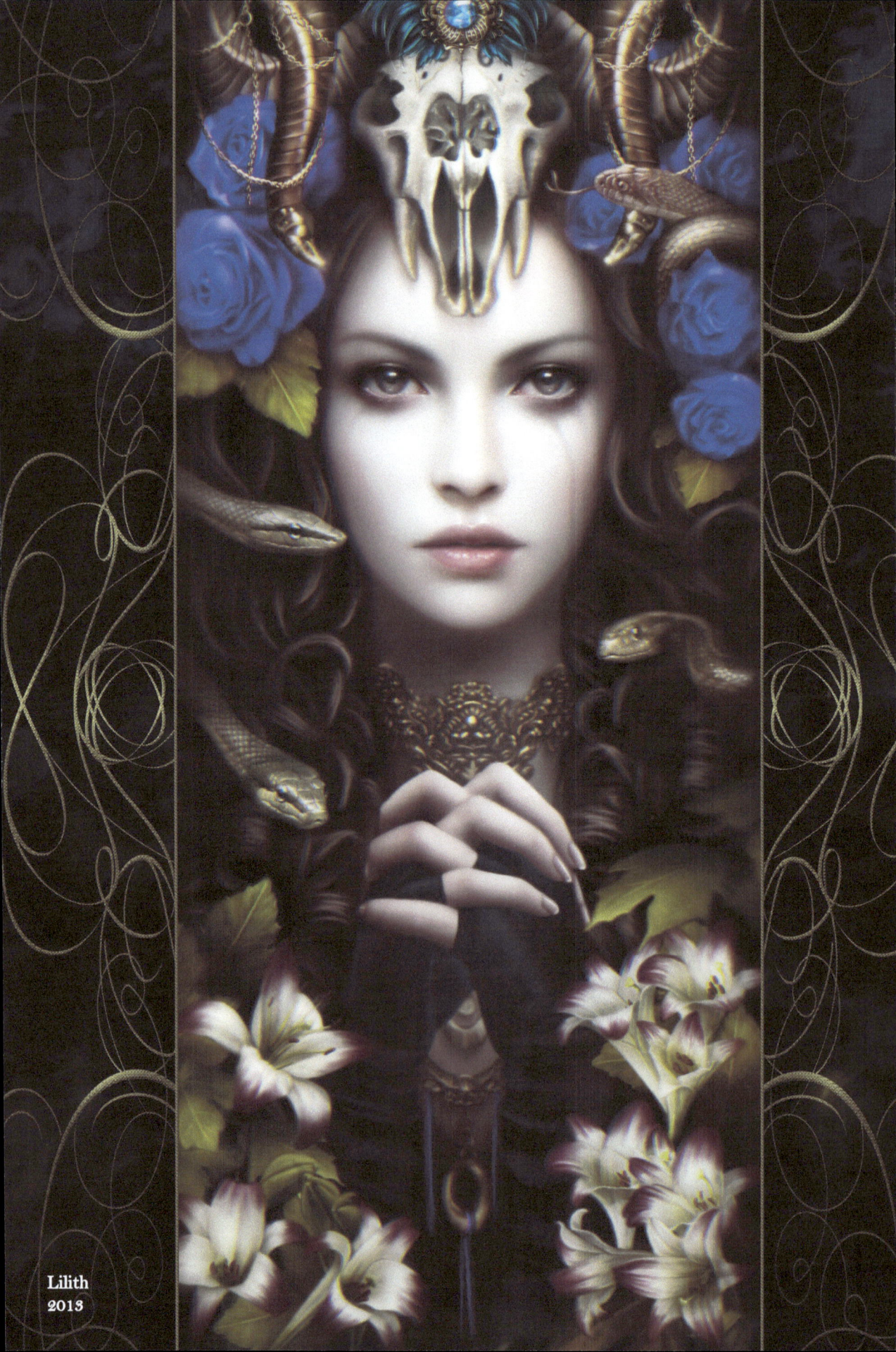

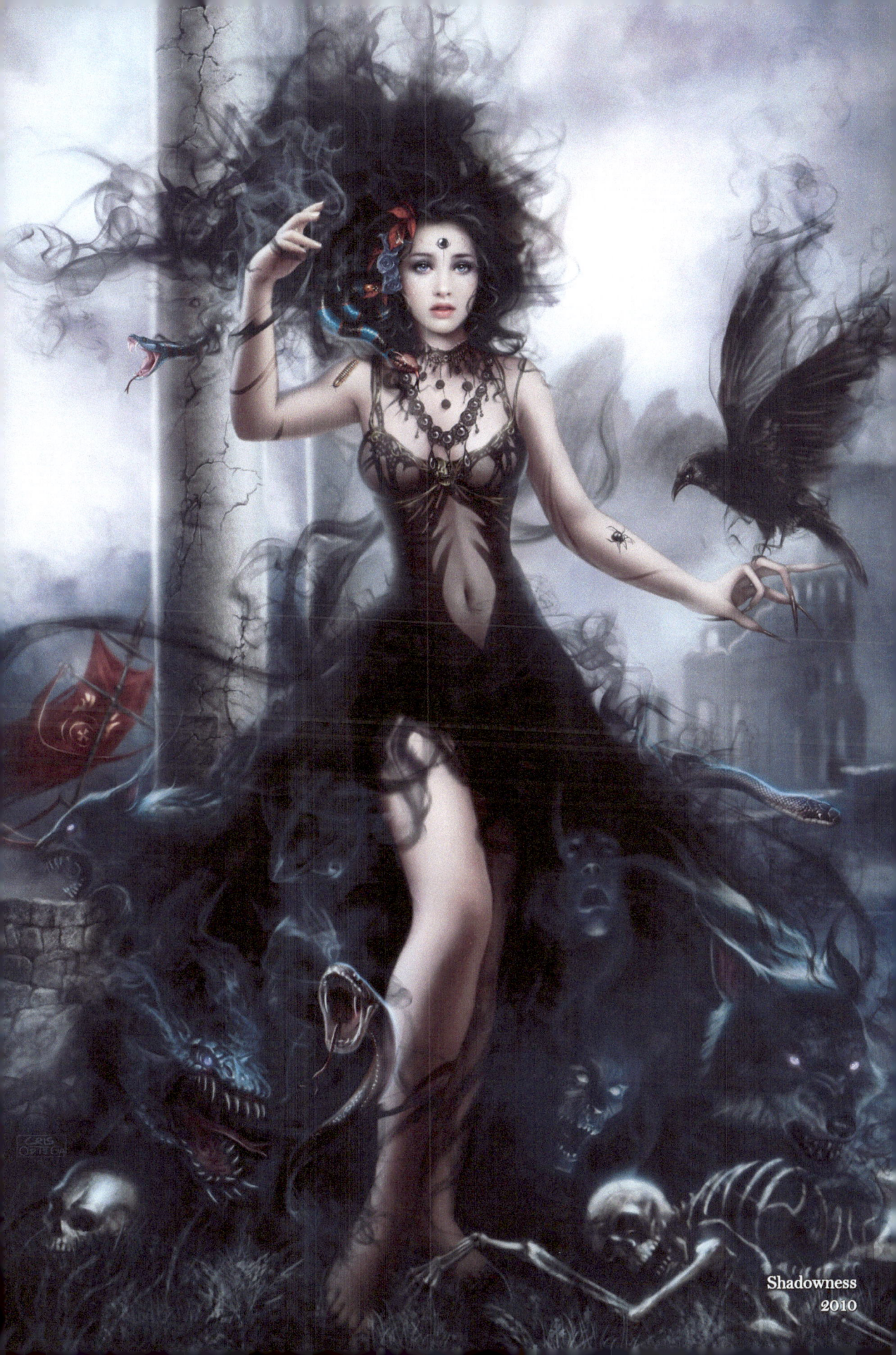

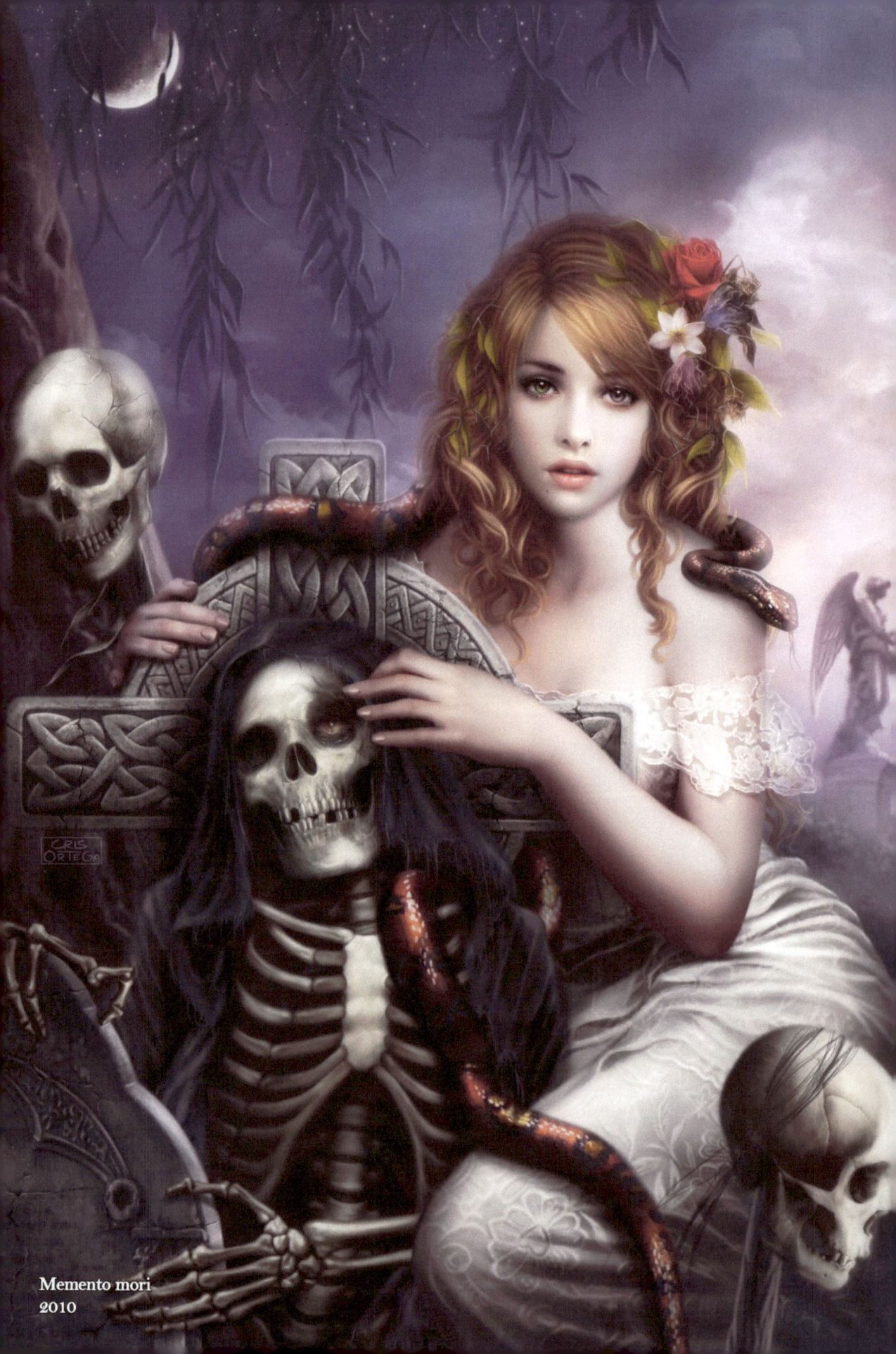

Memento mori
2010

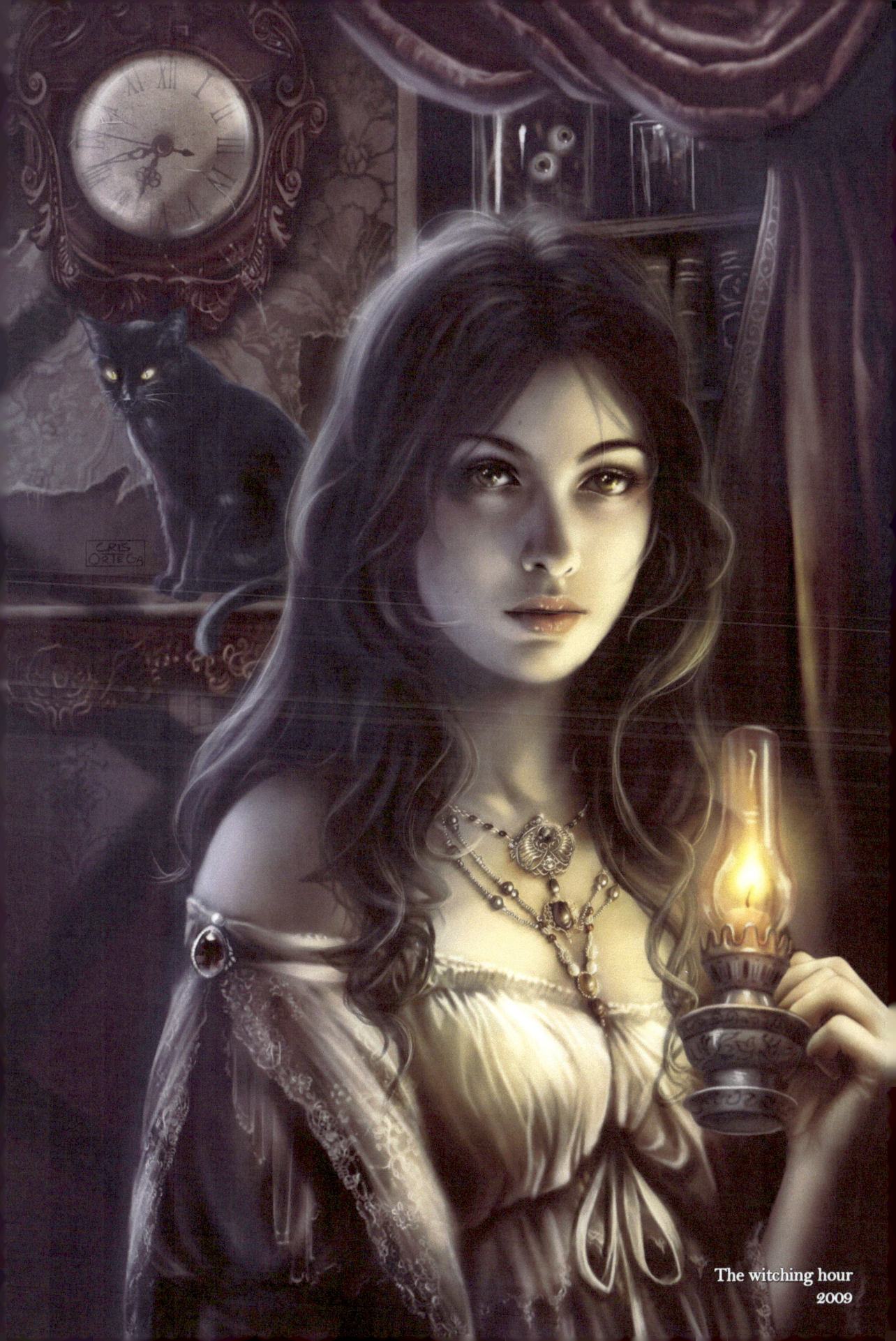

The witching hour
2009

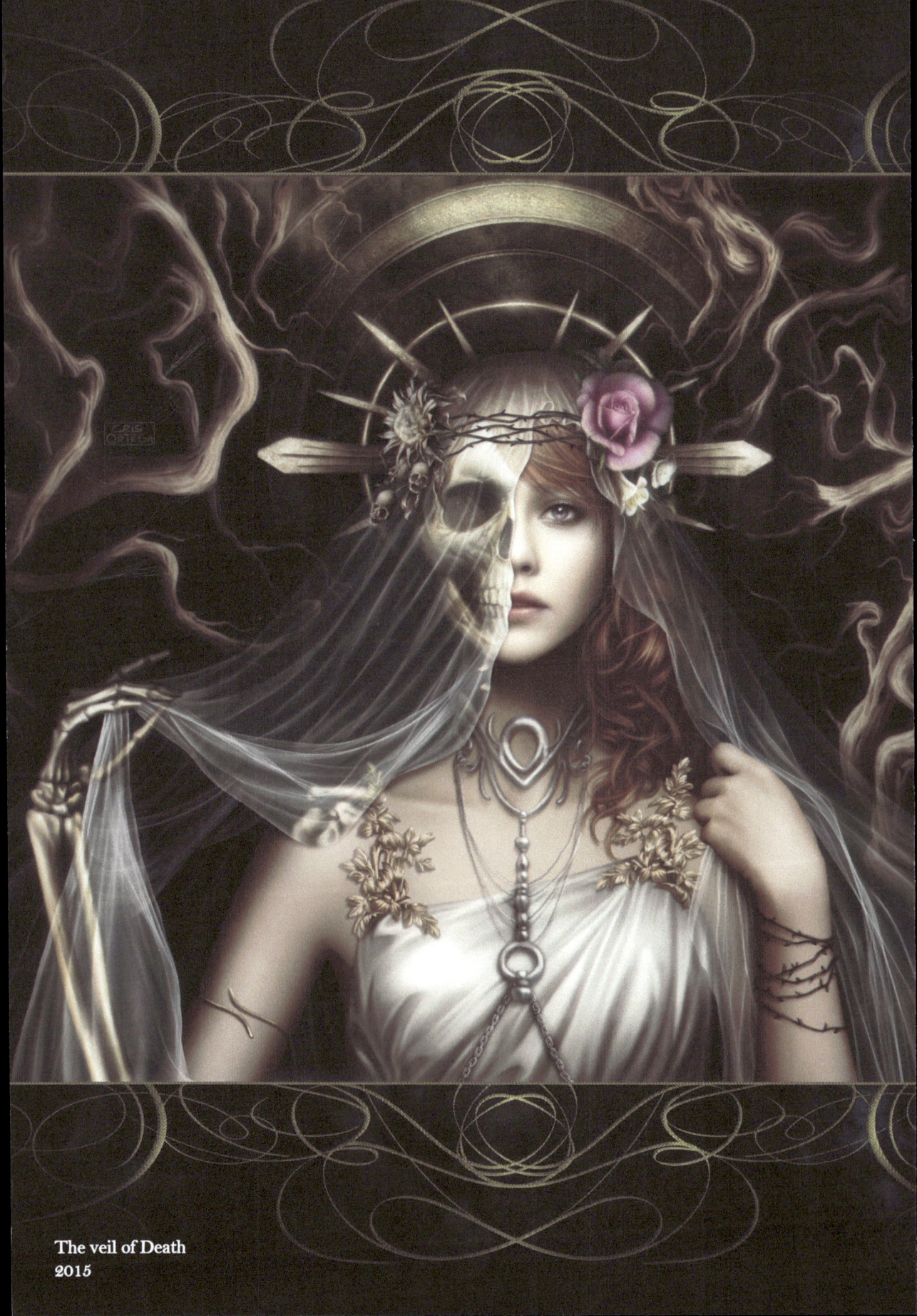

The veil of Death
2015

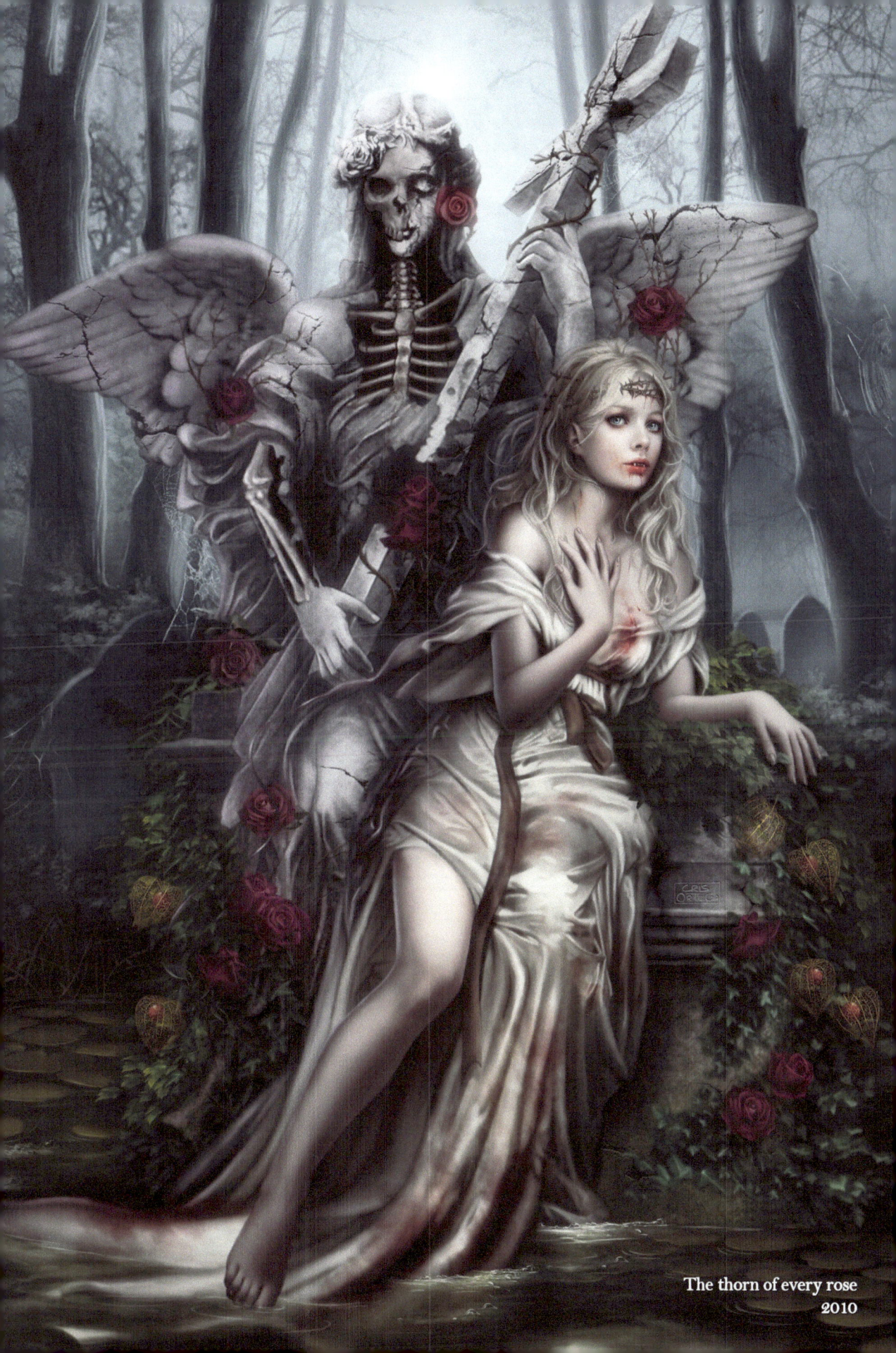

The thorn of every rose
2010

Author

Cris Ortega *is a spanish digital artist and writer who loves to work with fantasy, gothic and steampunk genres. Her publications include the trilogy of illustrated stories* **Forgotten**, *the artbooks* **Nocturna** *and* **Gold and Sword**, *and her series of grimdark fantasy novels* **The Shadow of the Red Crow** *(currently being translated into English).*

Her works can be found on book covers, puzzles, diamond art, games and all kind of merchandising products.

Autora

Cris Ortega *es una ilustradora y escritora española con predilección por la temática fantástica, gótica y steampunk. Entre sus publicaciones destacan la trilogía de relatos ilustrados* **Forgotten**, *sus libros de ilustraciones* **Nocturna** *y* **Gold and Sword**, *y su serie de novelas de fantasía grimdark* **La Sombra del Cuervo Rojo**.

Sus obras pueden encontrarse habitualmente en portadas de libros, puzzles, arte con diamantes, juegos de mesa y otros productos de merchandising.

@crisortega

@cris_ortega_art

@crisortegaart

@crisortegaart

WWW crisortega.com

shop@crisortega.com

amazon bit.ly/crisortega

www.ingramcontent.com/pod-product-compliance
Lightning Source LLC
Chambersburg PA
CBHW051051180526
45172CB00002B/601